Quality Management in a Lean Health Care Environment

Quality Management in a Lean Health Care Environment

Daniel Collins and Melissa Mannon

BUSINESS EXPERT PRESS

Quality Management in a Lean Health Care Environment

Copyright © Business Expert Press, LLC, 2015.

First published in 2015 by
Business Expert Press, LLC
222 East 46th Street, New York, NY 10017
www.businessexpertpress.com

ISBN-13: 978-1-60649-978-8 (paperback)
ISBN-13: 978-1-60649-979-5 (e-book)

Business Expert Press Health Care Management Collection

Collection ISSN: 2333-8601 (print)
Collection ISSN: 2333-861X (electronic)

Cover and interior design by Exeter Premedia Services Private Ltd., Chennai, India

First edition: 2015

10 9 8 7 6 5 4 3 2 1

Printed in the United States of America.

Abstract

Quality in a lean health care setting has one ultimate goal—to improve care delivery and value for the patient. The purpose of this book is to provide a blueprint to hospitals, healthcare organizations, leaders, and patient-facing workers with tools, training, and ideas to address quality within their organization. Examples from health care and other industries are provided to illustrate lean methodology, and its application in quality. The reader will learn how other organizations can improve their quality, know what their roles are, and know what they do daily. By the end of the book, you will have learned actionable concepts and have the tools and resources to start improving quality.

Keywords

lean, lean health care, quality improvement, quality management

Contents

Acknowledgments

The authors would like to thank the following colleagues who generously donated their time to help edit and provide guidance for this book: Wendy Blezek-Fleming, Shana Herzfeldt, Michael Radtke, Katie Roseman, John Toussaint, and Kimberly Wildes.

Introduction

Quality is a singular word that means many things to many people. In this book, quality will encompass all components of the patient experience, which includes but is not limited to the registration, building cleanliness, wait time, food, health outcome, communication, and care delivery. Additionally, the book will provide background knowledge on lean—a problem solving methodology—and tools, other helpful resources with real examples of how these tools and methodologies are employed in a quality department and integrated across an enterprise. Ultimately, quality cannot be done in a vacuum. That means that each category, unit, department, and segment of the process flow cannot be divorced from one another. This book will walk through the foundational components of lean and how quality management, tools, methodologies, and people fit together in health care quality.

Quality in health care can be defined by many entities—the health care system, the payers, or the patients. In 1999, the Institute of Medicine released a report that indicated nearly 98,000 people died of preventable medical errors each year; these deaths are preventable and speak to larger quality issues that exist in health care.[1] A more recent assessment in the *Journal of Patient Safety* suggests that the number of people who die from preventable errors could be 4.5 times higher based on analysis of other reports of medical errors and an examination of medical records for indications of adverse events.[2] In other industries, the quality of a product is determined by the customer; customers then choose whether or not to like or dislike an item, recommend it to friends, write an online review, and so on. In this book, quality is also defined from the customer's perspective. The patient is the person that ultimately should be happy with the health care they received. The patient wants to know they received the health care they needed and wanted, and that they did not overpay or get unnecessary tests or acquire additional illnesses. From a provider or health care system perspective, this means that quality is defined by providing the best-known current practices of care, promptly, and without error. Ultimately, what the customer is concerned with is the quality of care they receive divided by the cost they incur—otherwise known as the value. The equation determines value as perceived by the patient. It shows whether a patient paid for a Chevy and got a Cadillac, or if they paid for a Cadillac and got a Chevy. In the end, whether the consumer is shopping for a car or health care, they expect to get the best for the least amount of money. In order to provide the value that patients want, need, and desire, the quality component of the equation must be a critical focus.

Quality has to be inclusive of every part of the process which contacts the patient, because all of those instances are places where quality can be improved. Health care is different from other industries, like the manufacturing industry. Car manufacturers have to be concerned about the quality of part production, assembly, and safety so that the consumer is pleased and feels like they got a good value for their dollar. In health care, the patient is the *item* that receives services, but the patient is also the consumer that pays for the services. The patient plays dual roles, and in health care, the services can literally be the difference between life and death. This is not to dehumanize patients into products moving through an assembly line; this distinction is made to show how important and unique the patient's perspective is in health care and why, when talking about quality, the patient should be the focus.

Items as simple as the cleanliness of hallways, corridors, stairwells, and patient rooms *do* impact the perception of quality and patient satisfaction, and could impact health outcomes if the lack of cleanliness is extreme. Every patient comes with different expectations for their care, clinicians, facility, and more. For as many patients that come for treatment, there is the same number of differing perceptions of quality. From the health care clinical side of the continuum, a lack of cleanliness could cause injury due to falls, contamination of samples, or the spread of infections. When you view cleanliness from the patient's perspective, it adds another layer to the quality picture. If there is dust accumulated on the baseboards or full trash cans in the waiting rooms, how can the patient trust that you are getting the important things like completing the correct procedure, infection prevention, and providing the right medications at the right dosage? They cannot and that will cause anxiousness and dissatisfaction. The first thing we all do as patients when we are sitting in an exam room is to start looking around the room. We quickly notice if there are cobwebs in the corners or on the windowsills, or we see that something was spilled on the baseboard and not cleaned off, or that the trash is overflowing. To really champion health care quality you have to look at all aspects and causes of satisfaction and dissatisfaction. To really provide value to the patient, you have to be concerned with providing the highest quality possible at the lowest cost.

You will not see a chapter or a subsection that only discusses lean leadership. Lean leadership is about being involved, engaged, and visible within your organization. To describe lean leadership without the contextual background to understand their role and interactions with employees would be a disservice; a valuable resource to consult on this topic is David Mann's book *Creating a Lean Culture*. Leadership is the glue, nail, screw, or nut and bolt that holds the house of lean together. It is not one singular part of the structure; it is spread all through the large pieces and holds them together. This is a hard concept. In the early years of ThedaCare, leadership and the role they should play was a struggle. There was great work happening across the organization, but the teams lacked vision and did not know how to align their local improvements with the organizational vision. Kim Barnas, former senior vice president at ThedaCare, and a small team created a plan to close this gap by developing a management system to learn skills, and how to develop a plan to train and educate other leaders. A management system is very important for the success of lean and quality endeavors, but the detail and depth it deserves surpasses this book. Much of what accompanies lean leadership is how leadership interacts, is involved, and coaches employees on a daily basis.

Lean leadership is about doing things differently. John Toussaint, MD, says in his book, *On the Mend*, that leaders who think they know all of the answers, or are most comfortable leading from behind a desk, struggle with emotional capacity; this is not the right work for you.[3] Lean leaders are involved and engaged with their employees, floors, and units. Lean leaders go, see, and support their employees' needs, and they facilitate problem solving rather than running to the problem with a list of solutions for others to do. With a lean organization, you really have to flip the pyramid, where the executives are on the bottom and your

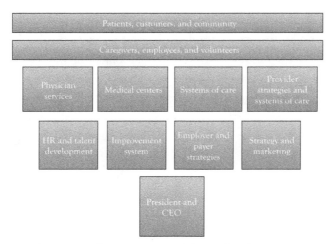

Figure I.1 An inverted organizational chart that has patients, customers, and the community at the top with the CEO and President at the bottom, demonstrating the ideological shift from a top-down approach to leadership

patient-facing workers at the top (Figure I.1). That way of thinking really changes how leadership functions within the organization.

The scope of this book is narrowed to quality management, but the quality department is a resource for every department in a health care system. We will discuss the essential components of quality management, which will include examples from other departments. Lean—including lean leadership—and quality have a symbiotic relationship that is essential for improvement and sustainment; quality work is focused on improving the current process to deliver the highest standard of care, and lean methodologies develop an environment that can sustain improvements. For the symbiosis to occur, organizations must understand how to build that environment. A house is not built from the roof to the foundation, and neither is a lean environment. The house of lean in Figure I.2 shows how you start from the foundation with standardized work and other processes that will be discussed in depth later in the book, then you build the walls with coaching and improvement processes, and, finally, you build the roof, which is what and who your organization is. The roof is called True North because, like True North on a compass, this should be the guiding force for the organization. The left pillar supports True

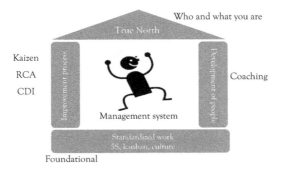

Figure I.2 The house of lean that shows the foundation of standardized work and culture with improvement events and coaching as the walls and True North as the roof

North through improvement processes; these processes can be kaizen, which is daily improvement work; a root cause analysis (RCA), which is really a tool to help a team determine the true cause of a problem; or continuous daily improvement (CDI), which is striving for an improvement each and every day to the work flow. The second pillar that supports True North is about developing people through coaching and mentoring. All of these tools, processes, and methodologies are supported by the foundation, which is composed of standardized work. This has to be at the base because you cannot improve processes without first having a baseline or standard for employees to work from. Standardized work is supported by activities such as the 5S is a process that helps create organization and structure in the work environment to improve productivity in the work place. Standardized work is also supported kanban—an organizational and inventory system that promotes efficiency by standardizing stocking, ordering, and reducing waste—and culture. Now, culture is included because people have to feel comfortable, safe, and supported in identifying errors. Activities such as gemba, which is the process of observing standards, can help support an open and transparent culture of problem solvers. This book does not give an exhaustive list of the tools and methodologies that compose the ideas of the house of lean, but serve as examples of the activities that support improvement processes or standardized work. The items and activities outlined in this book are those that directly support quality; however, there are many more tools used in lean.

CHAPTER 1

Foundation: Quality at the Source Gemba

The imagery of a foundation is usually built from a strong sturdy material such as concrete, cinder blocks, or brick and mortar. These things are there to provide a solid, supported structure that is intended to be supportive for life. During the lifetime, the structure could have many environmental influences that could compromise, degrade, and erode the foundation. Poor drainage can erode a house's foundation, a shift in the soil could cause the foundation to crack, or a storm could bring destructive damage. These environmental influences mean that the foundation has to be firmly built to withstand the challenges that could lie ahead, but there must also be diligent and responsible people who are there to mend the damage—to reinforce the once strong structure. All structures need maintenance, whether it is a physical building with a concrete foundation or a health care organization.

ThedaCare is an integrated health care delivery system in Wisconsin, with 5 hospitals and 27 physician clinics. ThedaCare has been on their lean journey for more than a decade, and former CEO, John Toussaint, founded the nonprofit organization—ThedaCare Center for Healthcare Value—to educate and spread lean through collaborative learning with other health care organizations. The hospital uses a collaborative care model developed through lean transformation and improvement, and they are also a pioneer accountable care organization (ACO). ACOs are a federal pilot program that reimburses based on quality and care management rather than fee-for-service (paying for everything done similar to how we pay for items in a grocery store).

ThedaCare has built a strong and solid foundation, but the organization must be careful as environmental factors like policy and technology changes, outdated facilities, employee turnover, and market competitions are all factors that could erode the organization's foundation, as well as the cultural, managerial, and organizational foundations that are needed to support the changes that have occurred and are yet to come. For this reason, foundational components like 5S, kanban, standardized work, and a culture of problem solving will be detailed in this chapter to help explain the necessary components of a strong foundation.

Gemba is defined simply as where the work is done. Lean terms are Japanese terms because lean is based on the Toyota Production System (TPS). Toyota developed this model of problem solving through empowering employees and by focusing on quality, the customer, and the respect for people. The term lean was coined by Dr. Jim Womack in the 1980s after studying Toyota's model of management and quality while at MIT.[1] This means that the gemba can be anywhere—the patient room, the supply room, the waiting room, and the pharmacy. The phrase *going to the gemba* just means to go and observe where the work is done. The purpose of gemba is not only to see but also to ask questions and learn what is done, how it is done, why it is done, and to identify waste. This chapter is intended to provide tools, training, and guidelines to help leaders understand what happens in gemba, what to do in gemba, and how to get a leader to *go* to gemba, so they can see the impact on quality at the source.

For example, at ThedaCare there were complaints that the stairwells were not being cleaned as often as they needed and that the doors were slamming and disturbing patients and employees. Leaders and employees observed the use of the stairwells to understand the current state and document their observations. They watched to see how often they were used, how dirty they were, if anybody came to clean the stairwell, how loud the doors were, and so on. After observing people's daily interactions with the issue, they would look for the root cause. Asking why does this: Why aren't the stairwells as clean as we would like them? Why is trash or dust accumulating? Why are the doors slamming? They would also ask, why is a very common tool used for uncovering root cause; this tool is usually referred to as the 5 whys. It is important to ask more than just why; you must delve into the issue.

Anyone, and that means anyone, can go to gemba and observe. In fact, fresh eyes can be helpful to see issues, or concerns, from a different perspective, which can be very valuable. The role of the leader during gemba is to ask thought-provoking questions of the workers to probe them and further develop their problem-solving skills. Leaders should not point out errors or defects and immediately tell them what they think the solution is. It is not the role of leadership in gemba to point out defects or waste or to give solutions for current problems. Leaders should just observe and ask questions that spur thought around potential improvement areas, and the questions should guide employees to develop their own solutions.

Checklists

Standardized work and process improvement are fantastic ways to improve items or tasks that are completed routinely, and they help promote standardized practice across the organization. Checklists are utilized as a complementary tool to standardized work, because they walk employees through the steps of a process. There are many tools people and organizations can use to search for root causes, improve work flow, and sustain improvement. All of those tools are not directly listed in the house of lean. Checklists are a great tool for the foundation: standardized work. Checklists are not intended to be for every single task, and should not include every step of a process. This could quickly create a 10-, 15-, or 20-page checklist, which would be ignored and would not benefit care quality. When you give directions to someone driving a car from point A to point B, you do not include steps such as get into your car, close the door, put the keys in the ignition, and so on. The same is true for checklists. Every miniscule step wastes time, because employees do not need to be reminded how to do things that they do daily, and it runs the risk of negatively impacting quality because employees may disregard the checklists due to the length—not to mention the morale impacts of walking employees through what to do daily.

Checklists are best used as a reminder that supports best practice. Labor hours are used to develop standardized work, and it must be evaluated and updated. Frequently missed items or items that are not routine are included in checklists to remind employees of the important steps that need to be completed. To extend the car example, the nurses, doctors, and whoever knows how to drive a car may forget a few turns or exits, which is when the checklists become helpful. They are there to help. Checklists highlight the one or two missed steps that can change a behavior, or to serve as a reminder for tasks that are not routine. A non-health-care example would be checklists in the airline industry. Pilots do not need checklists for routine everyday items, but they do have check-lists for emergencies such as water landings. This is not because they are not trained in water landings or do not know how to do so. The checklist is there to help pilots and other airline employees remember all the steps, because water landings are rarely done. It is because of their training and knowledge that the checklists are successful tools for them. Checklists are also beneficial for tasks that occur rarely, because if the employee only does this task a few times a year, it makes more sense to provide a checklist to assist the employee in completing the task. This process makes more sense than requiring employee members to remember the steps of rarely completed items and risk steps being missed or completed improperly. Providing checklists for rare items or processes reduces errors, because employees do not have to rely on memory alone to complete the task. These are here to support employees and allow them to spend more time caring for patients than memorizing rare processes.

Employees may be apprehensive toward checklists for a plethora of reasons. To get employee support and adoption, some call this *buy in* but that makes it sound like employees are being sold a product; leaders must prove that the lists are useful, will help patients, and mean fewer workarounds or wasted time for them. The best way to do this is to find an issue that employees have identified for which a checklist would be appropriate and to help them develop one for that issue.

Checklists are also appropriate for high-risk procedures. When there is a high risk of harm to the patient or the employee, it is important to have a checklist so that important steps are not forgotten or missed. For extremely contagious diseases, the risk of spreading the disease to health care workers or to other patients can be very high. A checklist can help employees with protection protocols, removal of protective gear, and decontamination. Checklists were first brought to the forefront of medicine by Atul Gawande with his article in *The New Yorker* magazine on the use of checklists for central line placements, which is then further expanded in his latter book, *The Checklist Manifesto*, where he introduces the need for checklists and time-outs before surgery.[2]

With any new process, there may be resistance from employees. Common reasons employees will cite for not using checklists are: it takes too long, this is *cookbook medicine*, I have never had an infection or wrong site surgery before so I do not need a checklist, I know how to do my job, and many more. It is crucial for leadership to communicate and engage with employees who are resistant to using checklists. At first, it is important to observe and coach employees through the checklist to make sure that everyone knows how to use it. It is also important to keep doing standard work observations after implementing a new checklist to make sure that the standard is still being met, and if it is not, then determine whether the standard needs to be updated. Most employees will be supportive of a checklist once you show them that it will help improve patient care (checklist manifesto author), but there will be opposition. With support, communication, and coaching, the opposition usually will become supportive, but if they do not, then the problem should be escalated before a patient or employee gets injured.

In the emergency room, checklists are used by the charge nurse to ensure that the crash carts are appropriately stocked and that the refrigerator temperatures are correct and documented for each shift. These are daily items that are checked; however, they can easily be overlooked or bypassed for other projects or someone else's responsibility. Checklists require an owner to ensure that the tasks are completed, and components obligations. Checklists keep items from being skipped. Without checklists, employees think that checking on items like the refrigerator temperature is someone else's responsibility. Checklists will have an owner, and although the owner can delegate the task, it remains the owner's responsibility to ensure that all the tasks on the daily checklist are completed. An owner is also needed for the surgical time-out. It is the circulating nurse's responsibility to call the time-out and walk the team through the questions before the surgeon can be handed his or her blade. The checklists ensure that crash carts and refrigerators are stocked, prepared, and functional. When the checklist item is observed or completed, the employee will sign and date to show that the task has been completed. This prevents the responsibility from being passed along, or employees assuming that someone else will likely get to it. Either situation can result in real quality implications for the patient. For example, if a crash cart is needed and no one had restocked it from the last time it was used, it can severely impact the care of the patient, resulting in possible death. If something were wrong with the crash cart, the team can review the checklist to see if it had been prepared, and if it had, it can help the team understand how to improve the process to prevent this from happening in the future (Figure 1.1).

When checklists are introduced, the intent is not to patronize patient-facing workers for missing these items. These are not used because workers have failed or because you have no faith or trust in their abilities; these are used to improve the processes that support their work. Checklists are there so that the patient-facing workers can spend their valuable time providing patient care instead of trying to recall the protocol for a rarely done process or during high-risk procedures. There are so many intricacies to every process in healthcare that management cannot reasonably expect that patient-facing employees will memorize each and

LifePak 500 AED DAILY CHECKLIST

Month__________ **Location**__________

DATE	TIME	AED: EXTERNAL INSPECTION WITHOUT DEFECTS	AED: READINESS DISPLAY READS "OK"	AED: HANDS-FREE DEFIB PADS X 2 PRESENT	BLS: BLOB MASK PRESENT	BLS: BMV AMBU BAG PRESENT	OUTDATES CHECKED (CHECK MONTHLY)	SIGNATURE
1								
2								
3								
4								
5								
6								
7								
8								
9								
10								
11								
12								
13								
14								
15								
16								
17								
18								
19								
20								
21								
22								
23								
24								
25								
26								
27								
28								
29								
30								
31								

***Figure 1.1** This is the checklist for the automated external defibrillator on a crash cart that has all of the components that must be checked—which day of the month it was checked and the time of day*

every step, and employees should not expect that of themselves. We are all human; that is why the processes should be built to support us. Checklists serve as a tool for reference to supplement the knowledge and experience of your employees. The employees still have to be knowledgeable and well trained to use the checklists, because the checklists would be utterly useless without their years of experience and knowledge. A lay person should not pick up the checklist and understand what to do because the list should not include each step; and since employees are well-trained professionals, those mundane, always done, never miss them steps are not included in the checklist.

The checklists are also useless if employees choose to ignore them. Employees have to know that the checklists were not implemented because employees are inadequate. It is quite the opposite. Employees are professionals, and we want them to be using their skills to the best of their ability to provide the utmost patient care and we do not want them wasting time trying to remember a process they do once a year, or asking others if they remember, or worse completing the process incorrectly because they may have overlooked a step. Checklists are there to help them do their job even better, but if they do not feel like the checklist is necessary or they are insulted by their use, then there is a problem. You have to have buy-in or they will be another laminated sheet of paper above a machine. A culture built on trust, transparency, and communication will help the adoption of checklists and ease the nerves of patient-facing employees.

Standardized Work Observations

An important component in effectively utilizing checklists and standardized work is to have routine observations of those tools in practice. Without standards and frequent observations, the missed items that should be included in the checklists cannot be determined. There has to be a baseline to build from. As many variations as possible need to be removed from the processes, so that no matter who is delivering the care it will be that same quality. Once there is a standard to compare to, it is easy to identify frequently missed items or opportunities for improvement. If you do not have a standardized process to work from, there will be too many variables and inconsistencies to develop a checklist that would be helpful.

Standardized work observations occur for two reasons: general routine observation to look for improvements and compliance, or defect or error has already been identified and needs to be further investigated. General observations occur to see how the standard is being used and to observe the process to see if there are areas to improve. Standardized work observations are another component of daily continuous improvement; it is the process of observing a daily task being completed while examining the standard work. For instance, the quality director could be observing a patient transfer for a person with limited mobility. The goal of a patient transfer is to move the person without any injury to them or to staff. The standard work would include that the appropriate number of staff are present and that the appropriate equipment (if needed), like a lift, are present. The director would observe how the team transfers the patient and if any steps were missed or skipped. If the staff decides to find an extra staff member to help because the room does not have a patient lift installed, the director may ask why the patient was placed in a room without a lift or why the room is not equipped with a lift. These questions, however, are not for the transition team but for the process. What process led to this patient being in this room? What process led to this room not having a lift? The director would not know why an additional person was needed for the patient transition without overseeing the process, and by resolving these issues, the hospital could prevent a patient or employee injury in the future. It could mean better care for another patient since an additional team member would not need to be pulled from their work. This observation is not an evaluation or critique of the employees but rather an assessment of the processes to see if they are working.

In either case, the purpose is to observe the current practice and identify improvement opportunities. Standardized work observations may resemble what many may know as an audit; the purpose is to go observe someone or a group of people work and to see if they are following the standardized work for the processes. The observer will usually have the standardized work with them, and they will need to have some awareness of the processes and type of care. Someone that has completely fresh eyes and does not work in the department could still be beneficial for overall processes, but they may not see when a standard health protocol is missed if they have knowledge of that agreement. These observations can resemble an audit, but the term audit carries a negative connotation that implies that it is one sided—meaning the person observing as power or authority over the attended and the person(s) being noticed have little to no input. This is not the case for standardized work observations. Standardized work observations are not meant to be a one-way street, intimidating, or negatively impacting the workers. Standardized work observations are supposed to identify areas of improvement and help those who perform the work.

This process is not designed to belittle employee contributions, nor is it designed to make employees feel like failures. It is normal for processes to deviate before a standard is in place; it would be unrealistic to expect zero deviations. With that understanding, the quality department and unit managers must approach deviations from the standard as a teaching and coaching moment, rather than an opportunity to scold. Deviation is not unique to healthcare; it is seen in the manufacturing sector as well. A deviation could be a customer service representative incorrectly completing the process of checking in a patient at a physician clinic. The representative may skip the step to confirm the patient's e-mail address at check in. A medical assistant may forget to address the health maintenance needs of a patient needing an immunization, or a nurse may not follow the standard for transferring a patient and gets injured. All of these processes need to be observed to understand if the standard is or is not being met, and whether adjustments should be made to help employees comply with standards or if the standard itself needs to be amended. Those observing must think about what caused the deviation to occur because more often than not the deviation is the result of a new requirement, new equipment, new rule, or a new employee member who, maybe, has not yet received training in that process.

At ThedaCare, a new care delivery model was implemented in clinics. Clinics and other ThedaCare leadership worked for three years to develop the new model with the intention of improving care outcomes and reducing harm. Clinic employees at all 22 clinics were trained in the new delivery model. But after several clinics had problems meeting their metrics, quality leaders visited the clinic and used the standards in the new delivery model to observe standard work and to understand what was happening. Through observation and asking questions, they had learned the clinic had the typical amount of turnover, but that meant some employees had started after the implementation of the new care delivery model, and they had not been fully trained like other employees. The employees who had been trained during implementation had fallen into autopilot. They thought they were completing tasks according to the new model, but it had been a while since they reviewed or compared their work to the model. That discovery also showed that standard work observations were not standard in this clinic.

To address the compliance issue, leadership challenged clinic administrators to observe standard work and understand what parts of the model were being followed. Hence, standard work observations became part of the clinic administrator's everyday work to keep the clinic from falling into autopilot. The entire clinic was retrained on the care delivery model so that old employees could be refreshed and new employees could be fully informed. Standard work observations are a lot like calibrating a machine in industry. A factory cannot expect a part to be made perfectly by a machine if that machine is never inspected, oiled, cleaned, and calibrated. If the machine is left to run without adjustments, the product will suffer at no fault of the machine. The same is true for clinics. The standards were not checked on and tuned up, so employees started using the standards that they knew. It is the responsibility of leaders to check on standards like this, coach, and seek adjustments if necessary.

Observations are very important when an opportunity for improvement is identified, because it allows everyone to understand the current state, and begins the process to find the root cause before making any adjustments. General observations are just as important, and possibly more important, because they allow daily routines, processes, and standardized work to be observed for consistency. Consistency, or a lack of variation, is very important for high quality health care. Quality management is about building a culture of high quality care and then consistently delivering that quality of care. General observations allow for small improvements to be made and for problems to be resolved before they become larger, and to make sure employees are adhering to standardized work before the variation causes an error. Going to gemba and observing is not a one-and-done event; gemba is a large commitment that is absolutely necessary for high quality care. Leaders have a standardized

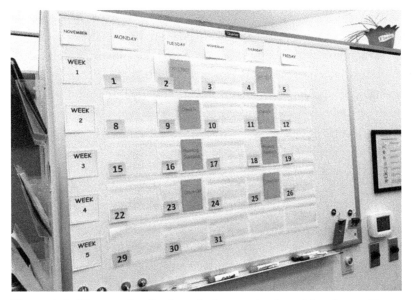

Figure 1.2 The standardized work observation board for the quality department. The planned observations and dates are planned out for each month at the same location

work observation calendar. This keeps track of when each location will be observed, and makes the act of going to gemba more visual (Figure 1.2). Gemba has to be done routinely, and the observers must really immerse themselves in the work to fully understand what others do on a daily basis. It is impossible to truly understand what is important in someone's daily work, and what needs to be improved if the leader has never been on the floor.

Standardized Work

Standardized work is the agreed upon process that should be completed when executing a particular task. The goal of standardized work is to develop the best-known way of completing the task with the highest quality possible, with least wastage. A key distinction between former and the typical orders given from superiors is that the standardized work is developed by a group of people involved in doing those tasks every day. The group may also involve quality coordinators, subject matter experts, or superiors, but the people who do the work daily are the key to developing and adhering to standardized work. Standardized work is the exact opposite of top-down control by hospital leaders; the employees, the people actually completing the work, create standardized work. Standard work is all about sequence and content, and to illustrate this ThedaCare uses a teaching tool called the standard pig that demonstrates the methodology of standard work by creating standardized work for drawing a pig. This allows employees to focus on the process and purpose of standard work.

For the standard pig, employees are given a blank sheet of paper and asked to first draw a pig in 40 seconds and then have the employees tape them on the wall. Everyone will see how, even though they were given the same directive, they all drew very different pigs. The next step is to give everyone two pieces of paper with a grid on it (Figure 1.3). One is used for the facilitator to teach the group the standard pig steps and the other page is for employees to use the standardized work to reproduce the standard pig. Here is the standardized work for the pig:

1. Draw a letter M at the top left intersection. Bottom center of M touches the intersection.
2. Draw the letter W at the bottom left intersection. Top center of W touches the intersection.
3. Draw the letter W at the bottom right intersection. Top center of W touches the intersection.
4. Draw an arc from the letter M to the top right intersection.
5. Draw another arc from the top right intersection to the bottom right W.
6. Draw an arc between the two bottom Ws.
7. Draw the letter O in the center left box.
8. Draw an arc from the letter M to the tangent of the circle.
9. Draw an arc from the left W to the tangent of the circle.
10. Draw an arc for the eye, half way between the M and the circle.
11. Draw an arc for the mouth, half way between the W and the circle. Must be a happy pig!
12. Draw the cursive letter e near the top of arc on the right.

Figure 1.3 The grid used for the standard pig

13. And finally draw two dots in the middle of the circle for the pig's nose.

The steps are numbered and they correspond with numbers on the standard pig drawing seen in Figure 1.4. This same process is how you develop standard work for health care, aviation, or car manufacturing. To make standardized work, employees start by understanding what is currently being done. The current state could have as many variations as

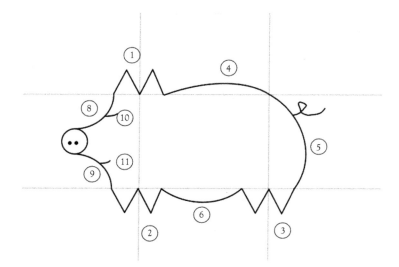

Figure 1.4 *Standard pig illustration with numbers that correspond with the standardized work*

there are people. Then after the current state is understood, the next step is to determine how the process should be done. Then the ideal process should be sequenced like a how-to guide so that anyone could pick up the standardized work and duplicate the process.

Stop Mechanisms

The ability to stop care in the event of a failed process or missing component is critical to patient care quality. Toyota has this function built into their manufacturing facilities. So that once an employee identifies a defect, they can stop the production line and prevent the defect from continuing further. This is the concept of building in stop mechanisms. The reason for this system is that the patient does not move forward with it if their care has or could have a defect. For example, if a crucial item from the chart, such as the History and Physical (H&P), is missing the care team, they can stop and address the issue prior to proceeding with care. This may sound like it would negatively impact quality by stopping care and delaying a procedure; however, stop mechanisms are only used on critical issues that have the ability to severely impact patient care and quality. If H&P is missing, then the doctors and nurses treating them will be working with incomplete information that could lead to a misdiagnosis, wrong medication administered, a medication reconciliation error, or more.

Another example of a use of stop mechanism is in the operating room (OR). If prior to the patient entering the OR a member of the care team identifies that supplies are missing, the procedure would be paused until the OR is equipped with the essential supplies. If the operation were to proceed without a fully stocked OR, the patient would be exposed to unnecessary risks, or if the H&P chart were missing the procedure, the operation would need to be temporarily postponed, because without accurate medical history, the surgeon and care team will be making critical decisions without complete patient information, which could unnecessarily lead to harm. Stop mechanisms work by allowing employees to stop the process when a problem or item with the potential to become a problem is identified.

In the OR there is a checklist that everyone uses, no matter the surgery, to make sure nothing is missed or forgotten. A member of the team would be responsible for going through the checklist, shown as follows, and making sure that each item has been completed before the surgery begins. If it is determined that the patient was not given antibiotics within an hour of treatment, then there would be a time-out to resolve the issue before the surgery could begin.

 1. Patient ID verbalized and correct?
 2. Procedure site verbalized and correct?
 3. Correct laterality?
 4. Procedure verbalized and correct including consent?
 5. Patient position verbalized and correct?
 6. Antibiotic started within one hour prior to incision and documented?
 7. Implants present and correct?
 8. Any special equipment present and correct?
 9. Team in agreement that time-out completed and correct?
10. Safety zone established?
11. Operative site marked?

Stop mechanisms are also called *pulling the cord*, because it comes from TPS. In their factories, workers would have access to a cord which they could pull if there was an identified error. This was to prevent the error from going forward and being passed onto someone else. When someone pulls the cord, the entire factory is said to erupt in applause to celebrate identifying an error.[3] At ThedaCare, there is not a physical cord that employees pull, but they can still report an error, and the process will be stopped and a containment plan will be implemented to prevent any further errors. At ThedaCare, units were doing root cause analysis (RCA) to try to solve specimen collection errors. Specimens were being mislabeled or lost, or the wrong test was being completed on the sample. This was even more problematic when it was an irretrievable specimen, meaning it was a tumor or mass that was removed during surgery so there was only one chance to get the specimen. Any recollection is wasteful and negatively impacts the quality of care a patient receives, but losing or completing the wrong test on an irretrievable specimen is worse. Units across the hospital had specimen errors occur, and they were addressing the issue locally; however, the quality department was able to see a larger trend of specimen errors occurring, which resulted in the vice president pulling the cord.

An immediate containment was put into place while the cause and a long-term process could be developed. The containment was similar to the surgical time-outs that occur in the OR, where everyone stops before the surgery to ensure that they have the right patients, they are doing the correct surgery, and that they have all needed supplies in the OR for the surgery. A checklist was created for specimen collection that required everyone in the OR to stop when the specimen was collected and to make sure it was the specimen they needed, label it at that moment with the patient information and tests needed, and then the specimen would be taken to the designated pickup location for the lab.

RCA uncovered that every OR had different procedures and practices, which therefore led to variation. Specimens were collected but not labeled until after the surgery, the label was not double checked, and the process for lab pick up was unclear. In addition, the electronic health record (EHR) that the lab was using was not communicating properly with the EHR that the care delivery side uses. The care delivery side would put in the correct information but it would not be translated to the lab's system. Both systems were from the same vendor, but they needed to communicate with each. The containment process will be tweaked a little as the problem with EHR is resolved, but it will likely be the permanent solution to ensure the accuracy of specimen collection, labeling, and lab delivery.

Escalation Process

A defined process to escalate urgent quality issues makes it easier to address the issue quickly, and employees do not have to waste precious time asking where to send their concerns. Urgent issues such as a malfunctioning infusion pump can quickly be reported, the action can be stopped, and the root cause can be investigated.

An infusion pump malfunction occurred at ThedaCare, where a patient was given a medication infusion, but the medication was infused faster than the standard dosage guidelines. An incident report was generated after the medication administration error was identified. In the initial review, it appeared that there had been a failure with the infusion pump, which prompted employees to pull the pump from service for further review. The error also spurred the need for an RCA to be completed to determine why the infusion pump malfunctioned. The first assessment did not show a defect with the pump, which prompted a review of the nursing process. A short time later, a very similar incident occurred with another medication infusion, which prompted another RCA to be conducted. The infusion pump issue was then escalated by the unit manager to the hospital vice president and chief nurse officer. This escalation led to a system-wide containment plan to limit any further infusion errors.

The plan ultimately led to the use of all of those infusion pumps from being discontinued. New infusion pumps were purchased, and they have built-in decision support and logs that record when the decision support was overridden. This allows the logs to be reviewed and, to understand, how often the standard is being overridden, and then to investigate why the machine is being overridden. The new machines offer poka-yoke in doses and rates entered based off a library in the computer memory, which is based on medication guidelines and best practice. Poka-yoke is a Japanese term for error proofing a process. The new infusion machines now provide another mechanism to help provide consistent high quality care and limit variation. This is an example of how one issue can be escalated to prevent further errors and harm and an entire fleet of machines to be replaced.

From the aforementioned example, the safety issue *could* have resulted in adverse medication reactions, prolonged hospital stay due to complications, overdose, and death. This book is not designed to get into the detail of developing a management system, but from the preceding example, the management system is how issues that should be escalated are identified. The structure and process to know whom to bring an issue to and when to do so should be established through a management system. The escalation process discussed here is what to do after a decision to escalate has been made and how that process works to prevent a defect from being passed on. Quality issues always impact the patient, but some issues, like the previous example, are truly life threatening. With a clearly defined process for escalation, employees can immediately recognize a safety concern and escalate their apprehension to their leaders so the problem can be managed swiftly with the least amount of harm to employees and patients (Figure 1.5). Once the problem has been identified and resolved, leaders can assess the situation and reevaluate to ensure that the intervention solved the problem.

To have an escalation process that works like the preceding example, you must first have the patient-facing employees who are empowered to recognize quality issues like a malfunctioning infusion pump, identify high priority issues that need to be escalated, and feel comfortable with leadership to bring the issue forward to be dealt with immediately. The escalation process starts with the identification of a problem; if your problems are only identified by managers, leaders, or the quality department, your identification of problems will always lag, and quality and patient outcomes will suffer because of it. Patient-facing workers need to be empowered to identify problems and escalate them accordingly so patient care does not suffer.

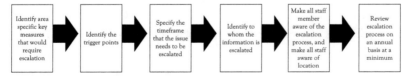

Figure 1.5 The escalation process once an issue has been identified, and it has been determined that there is a need to escalate the issue

Visual Management

There are two categories to visual management: the data management that occurs at huddle boards and visual management that is used as a form of communication to indicate that something needs to be done. The first form is to manage information at huddle boards, which are white board on each unit where staff come together to discuss improvement opportunities, issues, and achievements; the purpose of those areas is to communicate the information quickly so that any manager or employee can understand the problem and the changes and improvements that have been implemented. The second form impacts direct patient care, which includes visual cues to inform caregivers of specific patient needs or problems. There are many components to visual management at ThedaCare, and they are not tools or systems that are *just* used for quality purposes. Visual management has been integrated into all aspects of care for many reasons, however, despite the reason these tools were initially adopted, they are multifaceted tools that can and do support quality management.

Trust and culture are only two components to lean quality management, but they are critical to visual management. The word visual implies that one would observe the management, and that is exactly correct. Managers and leaders have to be on the floor to utilize visual management. Visual management is the crux of quality in a lean environment because it optimizes a transparent and open workspace and because it allows everyone to understand performance. Visual management is really leadership-standardized work that also allows everyone to see performances and processes. Leaders have to be out on the floor and in clinics to be able to observe practice, see visual metric tracking sheets at huddle boards, and to ask employees and units about performances and barriers they may need assistance with.

However, units and organizations that are beginning lean should be thoughtful about the difference between an open transparent performance environment with active leadership involvement and observation versus the traditional system of management tools. This difference is where a lean transformation can hit a barrier. Some people need help transitioning into a lean environment because many leaders have always led from behind their desks. A lean leader is expected to be where the services are delivered, observe processes, and coach teams to the standard. It can be a tough transition for managers who have not regularly spent time on the floor and with employees or have difficulty engaging and speaking with others, or leaders who are accustomed to solving all problems on their own. This can also be a hard transition for employees because they have to adjust to their managers being on the floor as well. It can feel like their managers are always around, looking over their shoulders, or critiquing or criticizing them. Leaders should not be blaming the employees or criticizing them; they should be offering support and asking how they can help, and what is keeping them from doing their job at the highest level of quality every single day. However, once leaders prove that observation-combined visual management works and that they are there to support employees *not* blame and shame, the process begins to work very well.

For example, certified nurse assistants (CNA) were complaining about morning vitals not being completed each day. There was no way for CNA to know whether vitals had been taken or not for a patient until after they logged into a computer, found their medical record, and checked. This led to concern from the CNAs that patients were either not having their vitals taken each morning or that they were taking vitals multiple times for no reason. After observing CNAs take vitals, it was discovered that there was no instant visual cue that could communicate to CNAs whether or not vitals had been completed. A flag was added to the exterior of the door with a designated color. Once a CNA was in that room and completed vitals, they would move the flag so others walking by would know that the vitals had been completed for that patient. Observation unlocked why CNAs were frustrated and how duplication was occurring. After implementing the flag system, the problem was resolved, frustration was lifted, and patients were getting the care they needed (Figures 1.6 and 1.7). All these visual cues can be seen from one central location, which helps nurses and employees monitor patient's status and needs with minimum waste (e.g., walking down hallways, asking other employees) (Figure 1.8).

Visual management helps with everyday tasks and care of patients, but the benefits of visual management are more *visible* when dealing with a high-risk situation. An instance that requires more protective garments, such as a highly contagious disease patient, means that there is a higher risk of employee harm *if* protocol is not followed. Employees are very

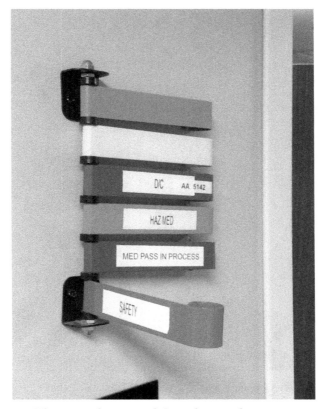

Figure 1.6 These are the manual flags that employees raise to indicate a need or requirement in that room for the patient. These communicate the needs to any employee who enters, and they have the flags labeled so that even an employee who typically does not work on that floor will understand the meaning

accustomed to going from room to room (of course with protocols such as washing hands and using gloves when required), but when a patient's illness requires containment protections, that is different. This means employees will have to stop and remember to do something that is out of their routine, which is where visual management can help. At ThedaCare, a stop sign is placed on the floor outside of the patient's door, and the instructions on what protective gear is required are placed on the clip by the room number (Figure 1.9). These two cues remind employees to stop and reassess the requirements before entering the patient's room for their own safety and the safety of other patients.

Figure 1.7 This image shows the manual flags with their surroundings and placement in the hallways. Above those is the light system that is used for visual management; each light has a meaning and can be seen from the central part of the hall (see Figure 1.3)

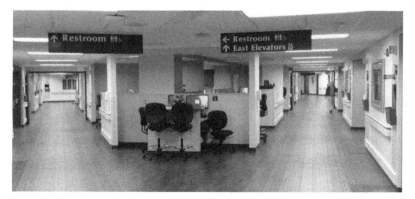

Figure 1.8 This is the central nursing location in between the two halls on this particular unit. From the nursing location, they can view the flags and lights for all of the rooms from one central location

Figure 1.9 The visual management stop sign on the floor and the instructions for extra protective gear clipped by the room number outside of a room

Organizational Level

Each organizational metric is displayed in the corporate visual room at ThedaCare, a room that is open at all times for employees and guests to visit. Organizational goals and targets are set at the executive level; however, those goals impact the entire organization. That is why visual data management is used at the executive level, and those metrics, targets, and goals are then integrated at the divisional level, department level, and throughout the organization. The work that is done in the departments, on the unit floors, and in the patient rooms all feeds into the organizational goals. The north wall of the room contains ThedaCare's True North goals. There are east, south, and west walls as well, which contain other key projects that are waiting for resources or employee injuries. The injuries are represented with female and male silhouettes. On their True North wall you will find five overarching categories: safety, quality, productivity, financial stewardship, and the patient. The patient at ThedaCare is referred to as *Lori*; giving her a name personifies her, and it is no longer just data because it becomes personal. It helps employees at all levels understand the impact of their work on the patient. Lori can be seen all over ThedaCare to remind everyone to provide the best services, exactly when they are needed (Figures 1.10 and 1.11).

The quality department uses visual management from all levels to help guide improvement work, observation in gemba, and support work with units and divisions. Visual management becomes a template for patient-facing workers, managers, leaders, and executives to work off of, and although visual management serves many purposes, it provides a key structure for quality improvement across the organization.

ThedaCare True North Metrics

Safety	2013 Target	Goal
System Pt Safety Bundle	82,865	0
D.A.R.T.	2.00	0

Quality	2013 Target	Goal
Preventable Mortality	TBD	0
30 Day Readmission	7.5%	0

"Lori"
Customer Loyalty

	2013 Target	Goal
Net Promoter Score	71%	100%

People	2013 Target	Goal
Engagement	39%	≥50%
Health Assessment Score	82.08	90

* 50% by 2017, 100% is long-term goal

Financial Stewardship	2013 Target	Goal
Operating Margin	4%	4-6%
Productivity	3.1%	*

* Greater than the annual salary increase

© 2011 ThedaCare   THEDA♡CARE   01-09-13 Rev: 1

Figure 1.10 This is the triangle that helps everyone remember how their work contributes to better care for Lori. It has safety and quality, people, and financial stewardship on the corners and Lori in the middle—because the patient should always be the focus

Figure 1.11 This a unit work board where you can see the triangle with Lori placed at the top and the local area metric written on the bottom so that the unit can see what metric they are working on, and how that relates back to Lori. Underneath the goal are the performances and targets. This is just one example of how the triangle and Lori are adopted all over ThedaCare

Divisional Level

The divisional level takes the metrics one step closer to patient-facing workers. The divisional level includes the cancer unit, the cardiovascular unit, the birth center, and so forth. The divisional leaders each have their own visual room where they take the goals for five key areas—safety and quality, financial stewardship, people, and customer experience in the middle—established by the executive team. These goals are created by assessing and identifying needs and gaps. Each division will have different areas of improvement, which means they can impact goals like the 3.1 percent annual productivity increase differently. This is another method of data and performance management that is very visual. The goals and performances are not hidden in an excel document on a network drive. They are openly posted and shared so everyone can learn and improve.

These boards with metrics and performances are in public places where employees, patients, and visitors are able to see what that unit is working on, and how well they are doing. This can be contentious to employees. Some may see it as leaving out your dirty laundry for all to see. If employees trust leadership and believe in the metrics and the work they are doing, then they know that this is an important component of transparency. Once they complete a project and improve a metric, they will be proud to show everyone what they have done. Even if a metric is performing poorly, having it on the board tells people that it is being worked on, instead of covering it up.

For example, the divisional leaders of the cardiovascular unit or emergency department will monitor their performance on various metrics like the time it takes to get from the door to the required procedure—this is often called door to balloon time. Other units will focus on metrics such as patient falls and decreasing the readmission rate of heart failure patients. Clinic employees will work on decreasing the number of diabetic patients with uncontrolled hemoglobin A1C (greater than nine), or increasing the number of patients that have received their Pneumovax—pneumonia vaccination or appropriate cancer screenings. They will find the areas where they can improve, and then those divisional goals will be displayed in their visual room. The divisional goals will not be identical to the organizational goals; you will not find *3.1 percent increase* under productivity. Instead, the divisional goals will be more targeted like decreasing overtime by improving scheduling for peak hours, or decreasing the time it takes to fully discharge a patient. These goals may not necessarily fall under the productivity category, but they contribute to improving productivity. By setting the target at the organizational level, the divisional level is given the freedom to choose how to contribute to the organizational goal, while also improving the areas that are important to their division.

Unit Level

The divisional goals are then passed down to the unit level. The work done at the unit level on the floor by patient-facing workers is what moves the divisional and organizational metrics. The organization cannot achieve goals unless there is buy in and commitment at all other levels. To continue the productivity example, the cardiovascular unit would take the goal to decrease discharge time within their unit. This may be a relatively easy metric to improve depending on a few factors. For example, the unit already knows the root cause of delayed discharge times, but the electronic medical record (EMR) does not signal to an administrative assistant when a patient is discharged, so they have to wait for a nurse or physician to bring them the charts. The solution is to make the information flow from providers to the administrative assistants faster and more streamlined so that providers are providing care and not delivering names for discharge. The potential solution could be an addition of a trigger within the EMR to immediately send an alert to an administrative assistant so that the patient begins their discharge paperwork more promptly. If the cause to the delayed discharge is unknown, the unit would have to do an RCA to determine the root cause or causes, or if the cause is something more systemic or labor intensive, it could require the assistance of divisional leaders or members of the quality team.

To do an RCA, you would use a tool like 5 Whys to determine the root cause. Once the unit identifies the root cause for long discharge times, a plan is developed to try the new process and to study and adjust as needed. Each unit from every division will do this process for all goals, and their work ultimately moves the metrics for the organization. It is easy to see how the closer we get to the patient level the closer one is impacting the measures.

Just like the organizational and divisional level, the unit level metrics are openly displayed. Units display their metrics and performance at their huddle board (Figure 1.12). Each unit has daily 15-minute huddles where employees talk about issues they had that day or the previous day, discuss improvement ideas, and highlight reasons for celebration. Remember, culture is a key component to make quality improvement work. Employees must feel valued or else they will quickly burn out.

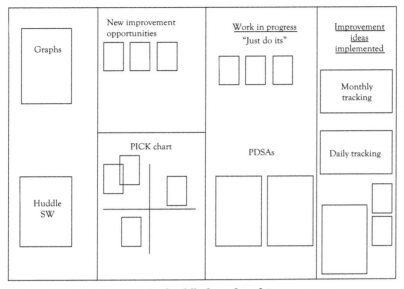

Figure 1.12 A diagram of a huddle board and its components

There is a huddle standard for the leader at the huddle board because the intention is to have a different member or employee lead the huddle everyday (see Appendix 2, "Huddle Board Standard Work"). New ideas are submitted via improvement slips, and then the unit team discusses the ideas and places the improvement ones on a PICK chart (see Appendix 3, "PICK Chart Standard Work"). The PICK chart plots ideas based on impact, difficulty, and the priority of the improvement. PICK is an acronym for possible, implement, challenge, and kill (or kibosh since *kill* is not a welcome word in health care), which represent the quadrants on the chart (see Figure 1.13).

The last part is very important to include because employees may have plenty of great ideas but not enough bandwidth to do the improvements justice. Pacing the improvements based on the time and availability as well as the immediate need is important. Some ideas are easily implemented and require minimum time, labor, and resources; these ideas are usually known at ThedaCare as *just do it*. Then there some ideas that are nixed for being too difficult and having minimal impact. Huddle boards are cellular so if something comes to us that crosses borders, for example, something that includes surgery, cardio, and more, we will discuss the

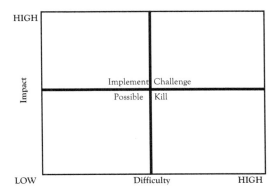

Figure 1.13 **A PICK chart plots the difficulty and impact of improvement ideas. An employee will plot improvement slips in one of the four quadrants. The top left quadrant is the highest impact lowest difficulty, and the lower right quadrant is the highest difficulty and lowest impact**

issue with the divisional or departmental leaders to see if it connects with improvement work in the other identified and overlapping areas. If an idea is chosen to move forward, typically the employee member who suggested the idea volunteers to take ownership, owning the progress, and monitoring it in future huddles (see Figure 1.14).

Let us move from visual data management to visual cues. The alerts do not necessarily indicate that something has gone wrong or there is an error, although that can be the case. The alerts are a means of effectively communicating a specific message. Units are all equipped with visual lights and colored flags outside the patient's room and in hallways to signal various status. The units were specifically designed so that unit employees could stand at one spot in the hallway and view the status of all patients. In larger units there is also a light that will indicate and direct the employee through which hallway the alert is in. These alerts are designed to be standard so there is efficient communication among the employees, and important information can be escalated immediately if needed. If heroics are necessary, it means that the system of problem solvers and standardized work has failed to prevent any error.[4]

Anyone that walks into the hallway may see these lights, but they may not know how frequently they are used or what purpose they serve. As an example, once a patient is told by a care team member that they

```
┌─────────────────────────────────────────┐
│  IMPROVEMENT OPPORTUNITY                  │
│  Name:_____ Date: _____      │
│  What is the problem?_____     │
│  _____    │
│  _____    │
│  Why is it happening?_____     │
│  _____    │
│  _____    │
│  Potential Solution:_____     │
│  _____    │
│  _____    │
│  True North Impact: (Circle one) Safety Quality │
│  Customer Satisfaction People Financial Stewardship │
│                                            │
│  Owner:_____     │
│  Who          What          By When        │
│                                            │
│                                            │
│  _____    │
│  Done Date:                                │
└─────────────────────────────────────────┘
```

Figure 1.14 The improvement slip available at huddle boards for employees to suggest improvements

are going to be discharged, the care team member will turn on a certain colored light that indicates to the unit clerk that a patient is ready for discharge. The unit clerk will then start the discharge paperwork for the patient. Once the discharge is complete and the patient is physically discharged from the room, another light is turned on by the care team to alert housekeeping that the room is vacant and needs to be cleaned. After housekeeping finishes refreshing the room, another light is used to indicate that the room is vacant and is ready for another patient. This now triggers readiness for a patient admission to occur in that room.

It is important to note that some alerts appear to indicate that something has gone wrong or that there was a failure. We want to stress that it is the opposite of what alerts *should* do for employees, because if the visual alert is communicating an error or crisis, the defect has already been created and now the response is reactionary. Alerts are there to get the attention of employees so that they can prevent a failure from occurring or to simply keep the process moving, therefore preventing a delay or point of dissatisfaction. The goal should always be to create no errors, so the alert system should be designed to prevent errors, not to tell you when an error has occurred. Visual alerts are there to preempt an error from occurring or to catch a near miss. When a near miss occurs, such as a patient that has a fall risk, but the risk was not identified until their last day in the hospital; the team will *want* to know about this incident because it was a near miss this time, but next time it could result in patient harm. Learning why the risk was not identified means preventing the risk from being missed the next time.

Another example of visual cues that are more adaptable than the built-in light and flag system is magnets. ThedaCare uses magnets to communicate information to other care team members. Both the lights and magnets communicate to many different people about what needs to be done or what steps have been completed. For example, the cardiac unit schedules all electrocardiograms (ECGs) for the morning. In the evening, the care team will place a magnet labeled ECG on the doorframe at eye level outside of the patient rooms that require an EKG. The next morning the EKG technician will bring their mobile machine to the unit, and they can move down the hall and know which rooms need EKGs. The magnets prevent the EKG technician from having to ask a nurse or someone else which room to visit, or prevents a nurse or other employee member from compiling a list of patients and room numbers that need an ECG. The use of one magnet decreases the amount of time wasted by the EKG technician searching for which rooms to go to or asking someone, or time wasted by an employee member compiling a list for the technician; eliminating these wastes ultimately means that the patient gets their EKG more quickly, their care can proceed, and their hospital stay is decreased—even if only by a few minutes to an hour. The magnets used are color-coded and the task, like EKG, are written on the magnet and placed on the door (Figure 1.15).

Visual cues can be used for other tasks or machines such as the use of a bladder scanner. In the cardiovascular unit, there is one bladder scanner, but employees could never seem to track down its location. Patient-facing employees were wasting time searching for a bladder scanner when they

Figure 1.15 The magnets used to communicate to employees whether a task has been completed for a patient

could have been providing patient care, which is not an ideal outcome. The solution was to create a clearly labeled designated location for the bladder scanner, and then have the sign the machine in and out so that the time spent searching for the machine is dramatically reduced.

If a patient is a fall risk, the patient will have reminders as well as the employee. The employee will see a magnet on the doorframe that says *fall risk* and there will be alarms on the patient to alert employees if they get up. The patient alarms are also there to remind the patient that they are a fall risk. Sometimes patients need the reminder more than the employee because, typically, at home or before surgery they could get up and walk a few feet to the restroom without any issue. Just getting out of bed to grab a cup of water is instinctual, and a patient might not remember that they are a fall risk until they have landed on the floor. The alarms go off to remind the patient to get back in bed, or it might remind them to hold onto the railing of the bed so that they do not fall after they have already gotten out of bed. These indicators can help prevent an accidental fall that could extend the patient stay or worsen their condition.

These types of visual cues work very well and improve efficiency when everyone is invested. All of the employees have to accept and use these lights, flags, and magnets in order for the system to work. The EKG technician has to trust that the care team will put the ECG magnet on the door of all of the patients who need one. Otherwise, the EKG technician will waste time second-guessing, miss a patient who needed an EKG, or waste a test on a patient who did not need it. Having an unneeded ECG is not an ideal outcome, and if it happens with an EKG, it could happen with a more invasive, uncomfortable, or expensive test or procedure. The employees have to trust their peers with signing the bladder scanner out and returning the scanner when they are done. Everyone has to use the visual alerts, and everyone has to respond appropriately to the alerts. Otherwise, they are as useful as holiday lights or refrigerator magnets.

Patient Level

The visual management that extends into the patient rooms is a mix of visual data management and visual alerts. Each room has a white board that the care delivery team will fill with the patient's name, the care team information such as name and role, a patient or family contact number, the care plan, and the expected discharge date. This component is more of the data management type of visual management. The information on the white board helps keep the patient informed and involved in their care, but it also serves as standardized work for the employee working with the patient, or a reference for anyone—phlebotomist, other patient-facing employee, or leader—who may need to talk with the patient or care delivery team. It is just another method to keep everyone on the same page and keep the care plan transparent for the patient and the communication flowing.

You can see in Figure 1.15 the elements of the patient's white board. It is a very helpful tool for the employee, but many of the items on the board are helpful for the patient and family. Quality is often viewed as a one-sided mechanism where the employees are in control, and they hold all responsibility for quality or the lack thereof. That is an antiquated view, though. Patients, for the most part, want to be engaged, and when information about their care is more transparent (such as being on a white board in their room), they are able to monitor their health status more closely and even catch potential errors. There is an entire section on the board devoted to family notes so that the patient and family can leave any questions or concerns they might have for their physician, knowing that the notes will be addressed. There is also a place for home medications, or the medications that the patient brought from home that were previously prescribed to them prior to their hospitalization. This is a helpful reminder for employees to know what the patient was taking at home and to help ensure the patient does not miss a dose of a normal medication while hospitalized, and also to prevent adverse drug interactions. This section also serves as a reminder both to the employee and to the patient to send their home medications back with the patient so there is no lapse in their treatment. Many things happen during discharge, and, so, it serves as another reminder for the patient and the care team to send those medications back with the patient. If you were to walk through patient rooms and look at the white boards, you will often find drawings from physicians to show patients what is needed to be done or what has been done to them during the procedure or surgery. White boards are a fairly simple inexpensive tool that are highly utilized to communicate a lot of information.

When a patient is admitted and is taken to their room, their nurse will do an initial assessment, which includes the white board. The patient name, date, and diagnosis will go on the white board immediately with the patient engaged in the process. These are small details in the grand scheme, but having the patient there reviewing the information on the board ensures that the data is correct and that the patient knows their diagnosis. All white boards, as seen in Figure 1.15, have the room number filled in so that patients and families have that number available without having to walk into the hallway to see their room number. This is another quality check for employees; when an employee walks into the room, they confirm with the board that they have the correct patient and room number. The care team will be filled in so that the patient and their family know who will be caring for the patient and will be in the room. As a care plan is developed, the board will be updated to reflect new information.

Kanban

Kanban is an inventory system that alleviates shortages, wasted time searching, and disorganization. Kanban can be used in patient rooms, in unit supply rooms, and at the systemic level. Kanban creates visual controls by organizing the supplies and making them visible to employees and stockers. Each item will have a tote or bin, and the bin will have a label that includes the type of supply contained within and the number of the supply that is supposed to be present, and at what number a restocking card should be placed in the envelope for the stockers. The restocking cards are colored cards that the stocker will collect. These cards indicate what supply it is, such as tongue depressors, how much we keep in stock and how much to order (if needed), and which vendor to order from. The cards are accumulated, and the supplies would be restocked. If the centralized storage area is out of a particular item, like tongue depressors, they are reordered, and the stocker will keep the kanban card so that when the supplies arrive they know which floor and room to take them to. As an additional visual cue and communication tool, a different card will be placed in the affected bins to inform employees that the supplies have been reordered, and with the expected date of arrival.

For example, each room in a particular unit is required to have two boxes of nonlatex gloves—that way when one box is empty there is a backup, and enough time to restock to prevent a lapse in supplies. There would be a bin clearly labeled nonlatex gloves and the number two. The kanban card is placed between the two boxes because that is the restock. This card will indicate to the user, which could be any nurse or doctor, that the bin needs to be restocked when they see the restocking card, since the card is placed between the boxes. The card will say nonlatex gloves, the quantity that should be ordered, and in which room the nonlatex gloves are. The user will then place the card in the designated area. The care notifies stockers that one box of nonlatex gloves are needed, and then the stockers will replenish the room and replace the card between the two boxes. This system keeps the room from ever running out of the supplies that are needed.

A ThedaCare clinic re-examined their stocking system after discovering that there was overstocking and expired items in 36 examination rooms and two procedure rooms. The system had been in place for a few years and had not been adjusted since implementation. The clinic assembled a team and began an RCA. The team found three different types of waste: too much stock, employees searching for supplies, and expired stock. Stock rooms may not seem directly linked to quality, but supplies are integrated into the entire care process, which means it is absolutely essential that items are in a standardized place, that employees know where they are, and that the items are not expired. If that is not the case, then there is a quality control problem which will impact patient care.

The team did standardized work observations and reevaluated the number of items that were needed on hand to be able to provide quality care without overstock or expired items. The standardized work observations allowed the team to identify that the current system was not working at the level that best suited the team and patients. In order to reevaluate the current system, the team had to use a tool, in this case 5S, to resolve the problem. In 5S, there are five areas: sort, straighten, shine, standardize, and sustain (Figure 1.16). In the sort phase, you are distinguishing

5S
1. Sort
Remove clutter from work space
Red tag items
2. Set
Everything has a place
How many?
3. Shine
Clean and repair
4. Standardize
Visual standards for who, what, when, and how
5. Sustain
Make it a discipline
Train
Audit

Figure 1.16 5S

required items from those not obligated to eliminate waste. Straighten is the component where the team assesses the remaining items and ensures they are in the right order for process flow. Shine is to clean up the workspace and standardize them by making the changes habitual. Sustain is just a reminder that the processes must be maintained to keep the benefits going.

After the standard amounts were determined, a kanban system was implemented in the stock cabinets. Figures 1.17 and 1.18 present the before and after photos. This improved the stock by decreasing wasteful overstocking or having expired products. The amounts needed were adjusted so ordering items per month actually decreased from $6,610 to $4,958. Postimprovement audits found zero expired items in the stock cabinets, which means better quality products, less waste from searching

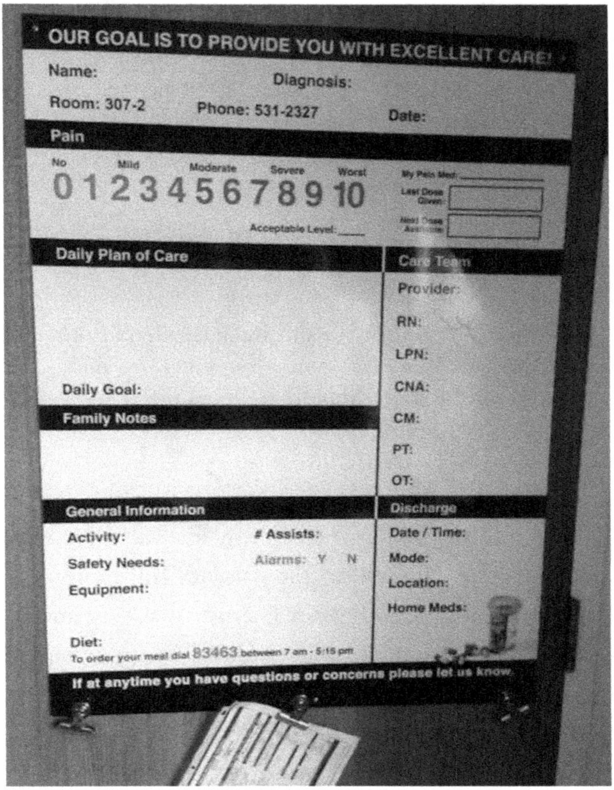

Figure 1.17 A patient board located in patient rooms for families, patients, and employees to use

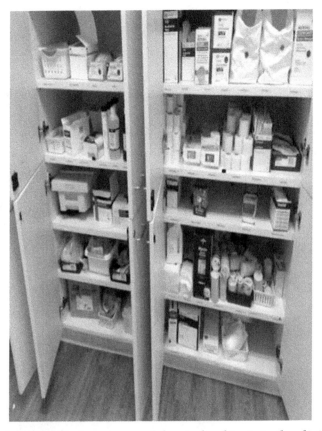

Figure 1.18 The before picture of the stock cabinets in the clinic. Items are clustered with similar items, but there are no bins or labels to clearly identify where items should go when being restocked

for items, and less waste from over ordering. All of those quality gains combined with the cost savings per month for the clinic mean that a higher value of care is delivered to the patient. This example illustrates how a system of organization for stock is a quality management concern, and how addressing even small organizational issues in one clinic can improve quality and value for the patient.

Although the kanban system is not directly linked to quality, it is a system in place that helps manage quality issues and provides visual cues to front-line employees, managers, and leaders, which make it easier to provide the highest quality services at the correct time. You can have

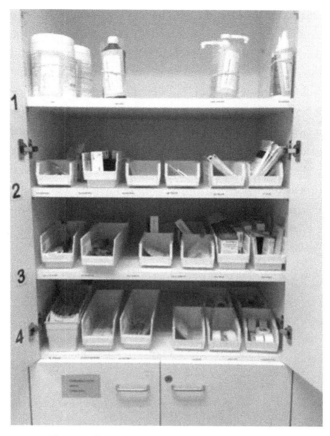

Figure 1.19 The result of the stock cabinet after the improvement project. The cabinets now have bins with labeled locations, and the shelves are labeled to create a standard location for each item, which is easily replicable by whoever restocks the cabinet or uses supplies

kanban without quality management, and you can have quality management without kanban, but they both benefit when they are used simultaneously. Kanban is a tool that can be used to improve and manage quality. These types of systems manage small quality issues daily and help keep the hospitals and clinics running smoothly, but they also allow the quality department to focus on other areas of improvement instead of spending time on supplies or stocking issues. Leaders are not wasting valuable time solving problems such as a shortage of nonlatex gloves, gauze, or any other supply, because those issues are preempted. Kanban keeps leaders and patient-facing workers focused on more pressing quality problems and on patient care, which ultimately leads to better quality of care.

The key takeaways from this chapter are to build a solid and sturdy foundation for the house of lean and many tools and systems that can be used to build standardized work. Building standards, and making the new standards habitual, is absolutely critical for other processes. In the next chapter, coaching and improvement processes will be discussed; these are the pillars that sit atop the foundation. Without the standardized work and items discussed in this chapter, the people development and improvement processes discussed in Chapter 2 would not have a foundation to sit on. For instance, it would be difficult for leadership to coach staff if there is not an established, agreed upon, best practice for that process. This is why the house of lean is built from the ground up.

CHAPTER 2

Pillars: Coaching, Improvement Process, and Data Measurement

Coaching in health care does not differ greatly from coaching in sports. A coach's role in sports is to help the athlete improve his or her skills through observation and targeting improvement. This may mean spending more time in the batting cages for a baseball player, doing more ball skills for a soccer player, or lifting weights as a football player. Basketball players spend hours and hours shooting thousands of free throws in their career, so that if they get one free throw in a game, they know the odds are in their favor, and that they will shoot the ball through the net when it counts. The coach observes the athletes during their training to make sure they are using their best form. This level of detail is performed for all athletes on a team. Championship teams are not created without countless hours of practice, coaching, and observation. The truth is, health care is not any different.

Leaders serve as coaches. Instead of shooting free throws, there are improvement processes like root cause analysis (RCA), continuous daily improvement, and data. These all serve as the pillars, or walls, of the house of lean. There are two pillars in the house of lean: improvement process and the development of people. The first pillar is the process and second is people development, but without both the roof will not stand. These pillars rest on the solid foundation and are methods used to achieve organizational goals instead of championship rings. These methods are not tools like hammers or a wrench that can be used without skill. These are methods that do require training, coaching, and continued attention; however, they allow organizations to achieve and sustain improvements.

Some definitions of quality, which are not all inclusive, can also lag behind best practice. For example, if a better practice is identified that provides faster, more effective, less costly care for the patient, it is easy for the provider, hospital, or health system to make the change. However, the problem occurs when practice is not aligned with what the Centers for Medicare and Medicaid Services (CMS), or insurers, will reimburse; CMS is a federal agency that is under the umbrella of the Department of Health and Human Services. CMS administers Medicare, partners with state governments to administer Medicaid, as well as insurance and health standards. It is much more difficult to change the standards of CMS and insurance companies.

A recent example of this is that the formerly known best practice for patients with diabetes or heart disease was to control their low-density lipids (LDL) to a number below 100. This is the standard that care is reimbursed for by insurance companies. This standard is determined by the best-known practice at the time. New research now indicates that having those patients on the right course of treatment—maximal medication management—is a better standard of care and a means to measure the quality of treatment, but payers have not adjusted their reimbursements accordingly.[1] The standard was created with the best-known medical practice at the time. The American Heart Association or the American Medical Society, or others, can release a new standard, but it takes time for that standard to be accepted and adopted. It takes time for payers to adjust their reimbursement standards, and they have to wait until the next renewal period so that they do not change the reimbursement standard mid-period. The standard that is reimbursed for is now out of date, which means providers, hospitals, and quality departments are faced with doing what is now best practice for the patient or doing what is best for reimbursement. This puts providers and reimbursement at odds, and ultimately, puts patient care and quality at risk.

The right thing to do is what is best for the patient, but sometimes the right things or current best practices do not align with what the payers expectations are as they are not able to adjust quickly to changes in current best practices in care. The dichotomy between the two puts patient care and quality at odds. These gray areas of quality and reimbursement are where it becomes very clear that small changes can have a large impact on patient care and hospital policy, and how quality management can help an organization provide excellent care by understanding the health and financial impacts on the patient and the hospital.

Quality in a lean environment, however, should be clearly defined without any ambiguity so people in the organization can understand what quality means, and take ownership of quality in their daily work. For a lean practitioner and a lean organization, quality is based on the teachings of Philip Crosby, a revered expert on quality, who taught that conformance to standards and requirements defines quality.[2] It is important to understand whose perspective quality is defined by; quality is either defined by the patient or by the patient's perspective, not by the person delivering care. In Crosby's model of quality, the goal is to accept no defects, create zero defects, and pass along zero defects. The only component truly missing from Crosby's model of quality that is present in a lean environment is the addition and importance of culture and leadership in quality. The reason we include culture and leadership is because we feel that without a truly open and supportive work environment, it is impossible to achieve the zero defect goals Crosby defines. We include both culture and leadership because workers have to feel safe and have no barriers in reporting defects, errors, or near misses. If the culture is not free, open, and supportive and the leadership is not supportive and engaged, then errors will be created, not reported, not resolved, and passed on.

This defect cycle will make employees feel helpless because they are unable to have a positive impact on their work and their work processes. This issue comes back to a core lean principle in that we must have respect for all employees. If the organization is not listening to employees, or employees feel like the organization does not act or follow through on ideas, complaints, or issues, then the message that is sent to employees is very clear—they do not matter. This is top-down, autocratic leadership, and it is toxic for quality.

A lean culture is one where every employee is empowered to help *identify* problems and make suggestions for their improvement without fear of reprimand. The entire culture must fundamentally change to one that embraces transparent reporting of errors and defects, so that the processes that created the errors can be improved. Lean culture requires that every employee change the way they approach their work; everyone must move past the "this is how we have always done it" mentality, and embrace critical thinking and continuous improvement and incorporate that into their work on a daily basis. We cannot stress the importance of engaging every patient facing worker. The workers are the gears in the machine that keep the whole hospital or clinic going. They have to adopt this way of thinking and the problem-solving tools so that they can improve their daily workflow and patient care. Organizations must be warned that as employees begin to trust leaders, feel more comfortable reporting errors, and identify defects, there will be a rise in incident reports, and numbers will look as though they are getting worse. This is not because processes have stopped working; this happens because processes that have always underperformed, or required workarounds by patient-facing employees, are now being honestly reported. These defects, errors, and near misses should be celebrated, but not because they happened but rather because employees identified them. In health care, and in quality work, it is easy to move on to the next improvement and skip over celebrating a success. It is important to celebrate because it contributes to a culture of reporting, providing positive reinforcement, and showing employees that they are valued.

In health care, celebrations can be overlooked because once an issue is resolved it is easy to just move on to the next improvement project. One example of how this was done at ThedaCare was by a cardiac unit that created a large tree in their hallway. The tree, its leaves, branches, and roots were all improvement ideas the team had identified. This served as a way to recognize and celebrate all of the ideas that had been identified, and it was displayed in the hallway so the entire unit, other units passing through, leadership, and patients could stop and see. The original tree (Figure 2.1) is now framed and permanently hung in the unit, but the team continues to work on new murals to celebrate.

Every employee, which includes managers, directors, vice presidents, presidents, and board members, has to believe in engaging and empowering employees to identify and solve problems. The work environment cannot be fully open and transparent until every employee has accepted their responsibility to be a problem solver *and* is supported by management to be a creative, inventive problem solver. This is hard to do but having leaders that have emotional intelligence, humility, and are able to recognize that employees will often have the best answer to the problem.

Figure 2.1 The tree that was developed from completed improvement ideas of the employees to show how small improvements across a unit can come together to have a large impact

These characteristics help reinforce problem solving. Crosby was moving in the right direction when he proposed that management and leadership must begin participating rather than supporting,[3] but he never quite made the jump that we feel is absolutely essential. In a lean culture, leadership must be engaged and willing to participate in the daily work and the improvement process. As Crosby said, leaders should participate in the work of others rather than supporting their work from behind a desk or an office door. Different industries have different cultures that may—for better or worse—be accepted. In the medical field, physicians are taught to be autocratic decision makers, and that mentality can lead to undesirable encounters with other medical professionals. Participation cannot be an "I-tell-you-how-it's-going-to-be" scenario, and it does not mean belittling staff or using your position or title as a reason for others to listen to you. Participating also does not mean developing every single solution; rather, it means being on the floor, observing the work, looking for gaps, and, most importantly, facilitating the employees to find creative solutions to improve their work or identify new areas of improvement. A lean cultural transformation cannot occur without active and engaged leaders, and leaders cannot be engaged if they are hidden in an office all day.

Lean culture is an essential component of quality; without the cultural component, lean thinking can only do so much. By this, we mean that an exceptional employee, for instance, an emergency room nurse, could identify a problem, and by learning about why the problem exists, they can identify the root cause, find a process improvement, or create a standardized process where one did not previously exist. However, if this employee is not supported by their emergency department director, their great improvement ideas would go unimplemented. Without leadership support, the improvement is never pursued, and the defect continues to exist. The department will continue the flawed practice, and this will eventually impact the nurse's willingness to solve problems. This ultimately will be seen in overall satisfaction and quality scores.

This scenario could have gone another way in traditional quality management. The nurse identifies a problem and tells their manager about it, but the manager entertains the idea and then provides the nurse with neither the go-ahead to move forward nor any support. Put yourself in the nurse's position; why would you continue to identify areas of improvement and develop a solution if you know your superiors will not be excited and work to implement the improvement across the department? If an employee had an easy improvement idea and hits a dead end with no support from leadership, then how is it not feasible to expect employees to accurately report errors in that environment? It is easy to see how this scenario quickly lowers the morale of those who have a desire to learn and improve.

Lean is best defined not as a tool but as a methodology that fosters critical thinking and continuous improvement through process-oriented analysis. Basically, it means that lean is a method of thinking about problems where the worker is empowered to ask "Why?" and the leader is expected to ask "Why?" The old adage "give a man a fish, and you feed him for a day; show him how to catch fish, and you feed him for a lifetime" is applicable to empowerment and lean leadership. Leaders could give the answers (or what they perceive to be answers), or they can teach their employees how to be empowered to solve problems and find the answers. It is a structured way of looking at a problem and asking the following: Why is this a problem? Why did the problem start? Why was there not a process in place to prevent this problem? Lean is not a set of tools to fix problems, but rather a method of thinking that can be applied to all work to improve efficiency, decrease errors, and—in health care—provide higher value care to the patient. Many people, even lean practitioners, confuse lean to be a toolbox where you can find a problem and immediately find an Excel worksheet or other document that will solve the problem. There are tools that facilitate lean thinking. These tools help cultivate problem solving to yield results, but the culture of the organization must be one where *everyone* feels empowered to identify and solve problems.

In order to apply lean methodology appropriately and make improvements, an organization must have actionable data. Lean requires that improvements and experiments should only be done once a problem is truly identified, studied, and well understood, which means diving into the data to learn *why* that problem exists, so appropriate countermeasures can be developed and tested.

Measuring Quality

The standard definition of quality, which is conformance to standards and requirements with the goal of zero defects, can be used to assess almost every component of health care from patient-registration employee to health outcomes. Process measures such as completing the appropriate protocol for a patient can be measured, as well as health outcomes, door to doctor times (how long it takes to see a doctor from the moment a patient walks in), patient satisfaction with registration, and more; however, quality measures fall into two main categories: process quality and patient satisfaction. The patient satisfaction survey used at ThedaCare contains multiple choice questions that ask patients if they felt their nurses listened, or if the doctors treated them with courtesy and respect; the survey also has questions that ask patients to rate their interactions with nurses, their wait times, and, even about, their meals. These are things that may not seem directly related to care in a traditional sense. For instance, if a patient is being treated for a broken neck, the courtesy of their doctor or the quality of their chicken salad wrap may not be important, but when it comes to quality in a lean organization, those are *all* points at which the system interacts with the patient's episode of care, and they are all areas where improvement can be made.

Surveys also provide room for comments to further explain positive or negative feedback. This seems like an obvious component to include, but it should be highlighted, because it can provide managers and leaders with a clearer picture of what went well and what did not go well, and how the team can learn from that encounter. Sometimes these freestyle responses provide the *why* behind the ratings. Surveys for these purposes usually contain about 40 questions. The questions cover topics like patient demographics, patient experience with all points of care—clerks, receptionists, clinicians, nurses. Patient experience includes how they felt during the interaction, ease of contacting the office or provider, the ease of asking questions, and how well information was explained to them and more.

Although all of the measurable components of quality like wait times, test results, and medications errors are intrinsically linked, since they are all part of the continuum of care, the expectations from different stakeholders regarding the measurements vary greatly. In health care, stakeholders can be the federal government, the state government, other state oversight, or other quality agencies such as the Wisconsin Collaborative for Healthcare Quality, the insurer, the hospital, the clinic, the physician, the patient, the family, and many others. The federal government, specifically CMS, expects certain processes to occur when treating certain conditions such as pneumonia or congestive heart failure. For instance, a patient who presents with pneumonia must have blood cultures taken in the emergency department prior to getting antibiotics, or for a patient with a heart attack, they must have had an aspirin 24 hours before their arrival to the emergency department or within 24 hours of their arrival to the hospital. These are known as core measures—specific items that CMS expects to occur for each diagnosis. Core measures, data collection, began in 2001 to measure compliance with current best practice, as defined by a group of stakeholders in health care, to ensure best patient care. Initially, the core measures were just for heart failure and acute myocardial infarction, but now there are 14 CMS core measures that hospitals have to collect and report data on.

A patient may not be aware of small process measures that maintain health care quality, such as checking the medical refrigerator temperature twice a day, because these processes are usually behind the scenes, and the patient does not come in direct contact with them. Patients may understand the required sequential step of needing a blood culture drawn before getting their antibiotic started, or that after 24 hours they should have their Foley catheter removed in order to decrease their risk of a urinary tract infection, but patients are also going to expect the right process to be the standard. They expect health care workers to take the right steps to ensure that they are receiving the best care. Patients and their families will not likely care whether the box for blood culture was checked off on the checklist before they got their antibiotics; the patient and their family care that the patient was treated quickly and appropriately and received the appropriate antibiotic for their infection as quickly as possible. A patient cares about how they are treated by employees, nurses, and physicians; the timeliness of their care; how attentive employees were to their needs; how well their health care dollars were used in the management of their care; and finally, and probably most importantly to the patient, that they feel better.

Appropriately completing process measures can and does directly impact a patient's care, but those are "behind the scenes" components of health care that patients usually do not see or think about unless something goes wrong. However, to meet and exceed the expectations of all stakeholders (with the patient being the top priority), all measurements of quality—process and satisfaction—must be measured, collected, and analyzed to provide quality patient care.

Press Ganey

ThedaCare and many other hospitals partner with Press Ganey to understand processes and improve the patient satisfaction aspects of quality. Press Ganey is a company that serves as a partner in improving and understanding patient care with the ultimate goal of reducing patient suffering.[4]

This type of measurement is not intended to do more than spur "smile campaigns" where hospital employees are encouraged to always smile or greet the patient at every encounter. Positive attitudes and polite and courteous behaviors from employees are valued by patients. Press Ganey is used to get data on how patients want to be treated and to identify gaps in the care they received and the care they want and deserve. To achieve this goal, Press Ganey manages surveys that include questions required by CMS, as well as questions targeted specifically at patient satisfaction, and questions that dive into the reasons for the patient's satisfaction or dissatisfaction. These questions are chosen based on the priorities of the hospital; this may mean wait times are focused on if that has been in an issue, or there may be questions added to get to the root cause of patient dissatisfaction.

In addition to providing survey data, Press Ganey offers advice and strategies based on best-known practices to improve measures. Press Ganey measures the following domains: communication, care team, pain management, access, timeliness, and how quickly the patients are seen by their provider. At ThedaCare, one of the most common complaints received is about wait times. This type of information guides quality improvement work and helps target RCA to look into *why* wait times exist and what causes the dissatisfaction for patients. One main reason that patients do not like wait time prior to seeing the doctor, or for imaging, or at any point during the care experience is that the wait times are anxiety inducing if they are not told why they are waiting. Remember, for most people, a doctor or a hospital visit induces anxiety no matter what, so the fewer additional points of possible anxiety the better the patient experience will be.

To find the root cause for the wait time between getting an ultrasound and when the patient hears their results, the team would first recognize that this is a point of dissatisfaction that needs to be addressed. The team would work through 5 Whys by asking why there is a delay between the completion of the ultrasound and the patient's results. The reason the team identified for this could be that getting a radiologist to read the ultrasound is taking too long. The team would then discuss what reasons could be causing the wait for a radiologist. Those reasons are that there is only one radiologist on staff at odd hours, and that physicians do not have a way to know when the ultrasound has been checked and when the results are ready. The team discovers that there is no standard process for alerting physicians when ultrasound results are ready, and that there is often only one radiologist on staff during shifts. They investigate both and decide that the root cause is that staffing for radiologists does not match the need, and that a standard to alert physicians when results are ready is needed. This is a pretty common result from an RCA, where a lack of standard and a lack of flow led to wait times.

All health care organizations are required to report HCAHPS (Hospital Consumer Assessment of Healthcare Providers and Systems) to the federal government, which means they must collect consumer assessment. The requirement, however, is just the tip of the iceberg in terms of information. They can tell you if people are satisfied or unsatisfied, but very little is given beyond that. Press Ganey is used at ThedaCare to collect the required information for HCAHPS and to find out more of the *why* behind the scores.

Press Ganey is also utilized to measure and report the Hospital Consumer Assessment of Healthcare Providers and Systems (HCAHPS) and the Clinical Group Consumer Assessment of Providers and Systems (CG-CAHPS). Both assessments are designed to develop standardized national data on patient experience, and the participated hospitals, like ThedaCare, have their data publicly reported. Although the surveys are used to meet a government requirement, or the process component of quality, they also help uncover the more complex component of quality—patient satisfaction. For instance, consumers can look up HCAHPS scores online. They would see that 73 percent of patients reported that their nurses *always* communicated well, and that the Wisconsin average is 82 percent whereas the national average is 79 percent.[5] Without Press Ganey, that would be the end of the information, but with Press Ganey the reasons for why only 73 percent reported that can be parsed out. They can ask more targeted question to find out what parts of the communication process could work better, such as medication direction or answering questions.

Without comprehensive surveys, patient satisfaction data would be missing from the quality spectrum. In order to provide defect-free care, a hospital has to understand where opportunities for improvement exist, so they can work toward the goal of zero defects. Patient satisfaction may reveal some defects directly related to patient satisfaction, or it might indicate defects in other areas that need exploration.

Creating Information from Data

Many measures are tracked at ThedaCare, but the data must be analyzed in order to garner meaningful information from the info for quality managers, unit managers, and others. One method is to create a statistical process control (SPC). What differentiates an SPC from a simple run chart is the ability to help understand process variation. The SPCs will also contain an upper control limit (UCL) and lower control limit (LCL), which are key to understanding performance. The UCL and LCL allow the plotted information to be taken out of the abstract and put into context so that the variation can be examined; an example of a UCL and LCL can be seen in Figure 2.2. Variation occurs, but an important distinction for quality purposes is to be able to determine if the variation is or is not normal. There are two types of process variations: common cause and special cause variation. If the trend is between the UCL and LCL, then the variation is considered common cause variation, but if the variation extends beyond either limit, then it is classified as abnormal or special cause variation, and an RCA—an investigation into the reasons and causes for the change—would begin. A longer trend of five data points in one direction, low or high, signals a special cause variation, which would also trigger an RCA. The pivotal point for quality is that employees

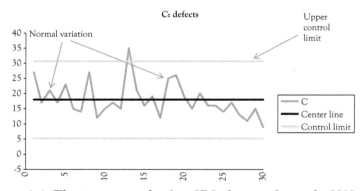

Figure 2.2 This is an example of an SPC chart to choose the UCL and LCL and the variation in performance

should be able to clearly understand normal from abnormal. Once they can easily ascertain that information, they can quickly determine what is performing well and what needs improvement, or even identify an issue early before it escalates into a large quality problem, hurts patients, or hurts employees.

It is important to note that this discussion of data is not intended to be a primer for data analysis, or even an in-depth discussion, but instead a background on the type of analytics used in quality at ThedaCare. Other resources will provide more detail on the use, creation, limits, and more. An RCA is a methodical way to understand the cause(s) for problems that arise (see Appendix 1, "RCA Standard Work"). As the previous paragraph explains, RCAs are not used for every issue. This method is reserved for problems that consistently arise, not one-time issues, and for sentinel events. The reason for this is that RCAs are time consuming, because the purpose is to delve deep into the cause(s) of the problem. The goal of any root cause is to understand why the current state exists, be it a wrong site surgery or employee that was stuck with a needle during a procedure. The key word in these analyses is why and not who. Figure 2.3 is a thought web that shows the process taken for an RCA. The reason you would limit RCAs to persistent identified problems or sentinel events is because small issues that can be easily solved by a minor adjustment in standardized work should be dealt with using the simplest method. Think of this as Occam's razor, the simplest method with the fewest assumptions and moving parts is the best method to pursue. More complex issues such as a five data points of below target rates of infection would require a deeper investigation, resulting in an RCA being used.

RCAs are a routine improvement activity at ThedaCare and are a crucial component to quality. All employees need to know the general process for an RCA, so they can all actively contribute to problem solving and quality improvement in their work and for their patients. RCA participants have to understand that the process is not to assign blame but to understand why the incident occurred and how to put measures in place to prevent it from happening in the future. The flow chart pictured in Figure 2.3 as well as the fishbone diagram in Figure 2.4 are fairly common tools for this process. Fishbone diagrams, however, can be very time intensive and can, at times, require more work than necessary to get to

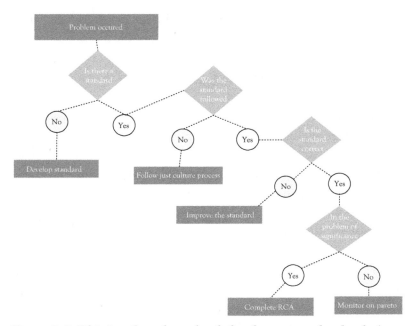

Figure 2.3 This is a flow chart that helps determine what level of improvement is needed for an issue

the root cause of the problem. Figure 2.4 is a fishbone diagram. It is called a fishbone because it has small branches that look similar to fish bones. However, it can get time consuming and even do more harm than good if people get too wrapped up in deciding if a reason is a second why or a third why. Essentially you can get *in the weeds*, and that can postpone real helpful changes. Although these templates are unique they are all based on the 5 Whys, which is a series of questions to ask why the status quo is the case. For example, if central line infections were increasing in a unit, the team would start by asking if there is standard for placing central line infections. Then they would ask if that standard has been followed. If the standard was not followed, they would ask why the standard was not adhered to and whether the standard addresses the problem. These questions and the tools based on these questions are intended to understand *why* the current condition exists. The key with these tools is to find out *why* not *who*.

SPCs are a tool widely utilized to interpret quality data, but SPCs are only helpful in showing long-term trends. In order to measure for normal

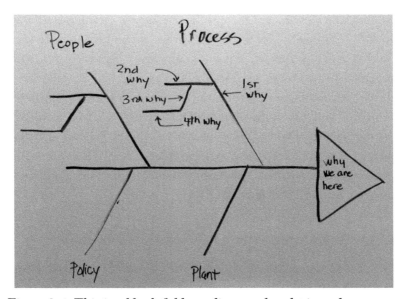

Figure 2.4 This is a blank fishbone diagram that depicts where concepts like the reason for the fishbone, the problem, are placed. It also shows where you map the first cause or why, and then how you break down the whys that cause the first why

and abnormal variation or to find a special cause variation, a certain number of cases or data points are required. The purpose of this book is not to teach readers about SPCs, but that it is important to know that there are different types of charts for different sample sizes and the type of data (discrete or continuous).

In addition to studying long-term trends such as average length of stay and readmission rates, daily measures such as falls, patient volumes, employees, and others are continuously measured. Physicians and employees use daily data to check on their annual targets. For example, physicians at ThedaCare have targets to reach for vaccinating at-risk population for pneumonia. By checking their daily numbers, physicians can see how many of their patients who are in the at-risk population were seen and vaccinated. Daily measures are measures that the work team is responsible to document on a tracking tool. These measures will have targets that the work team will be expected to make adjustment based off the information available to them in order to try and meet the metric target.

Some measures are tracked more or less frequently, meaning hourly, by the shift, or just daily—for example, an in-patient unit trying to decrease falls after it was identified that the team was struggling to complete their purposeful patient rounding from 12:00 p.m. to 3:00 p.m. It is determined that the employees were unavailable due to lunches and discharges during this time frame; the team developed countermeasures to address the improvement opportunity and tracked falls during the identified time frame to ensure that employees could get a lunch break. The daily tracking assists the team in making adjustments and understanding if they are achieving their goal of decreasing falls.

Quality Department's Roles and Responsibilities

The roles and responsibilities of the quality department are integral to how the department supports patient-facing employees, practice administrators, and other staff involved in the delivery of care across the system. The quality department should not be seen as an *outsider* who comes into what they are performing; in fact, the quality department is made up of a multitude of different staff with vastly varying roles and responsibilities. The team is all health care professionals with Lori always at the center of their work—be it facilitating a state audit or abstracting cardiac data for submission to a national data registry. Each of these roles is important to our system, but for the context of this book we will focus on several of these roles. The quality department should be seen as a support department that supports patient-facing employees. They are the eyes and the ears for the patient-facing employees because doctors, nurses, and other providers are focused on patient care. It is far too much for any one person to focus on providing the highest quality direct patient care while simultaneously monitoring the overall quality inputs and outputs and trends of the departments. Whether it is in manufacturing or health care, providing a high-quality result is the product of a team effort, and quality is there to support all the teams (Figure 2.5). The quality department serves as the connector between the resources and tools available and the operational units; they assist operational leaders to improve the quality of their process outputs, and the department may not have the answers, but they will reach out to networks and others to find the appropriate resources.

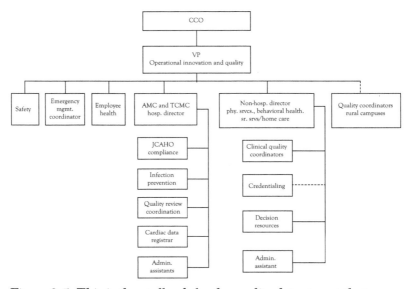

Figure 2.5 **This is the staff web for the quality department that shows the leadership and employees who compile the department**

An example of team approach to quality and how quality and the people within the department support patient-facing employee is the best way to demonstrate how quality supports the system from bottom-up. At ThedaCare, the leadership team asked the quality department to evaluate the True North metrics, which are the guiding principles that the organization has decided to focus on to improve quality and decrease cost for patients. The True North metrics for quality were focused on the hospitals and were not inclusive of the entire system. Isolated organization quality metrics means that the clinics and other parts of the system not included in the hospital metrics were, in a sense, ignored.

The quality director took this task from senior leadership back to the quality coordinator. The coordinators are responsible for many operational, day-to-day tasks, which include observing units and coaching employees. The quality coordinators then began to dig into their data to look for gaps in quality and combine them with their observational experiences and with feedback and input from the employees they have coached and observed. The coordinators and directors found a common theme, which would be included of the entire system—reduce harm.

Once a set of identified gaps were selected, the team brought them to the business and data analysts. The analysts work in concert with the quality team. The quality team can find gaps in reports and scorecards, but the analysts are the ones who create those reports and turn raw data into information. Once the team has identified the metrics they would like to include in the True North, the analysts are responsible for learning what is needed for those metrics, determining if it has been measured before, and whether or not there is a sound method of measurement. One of the tools used in the process is a grid, referred to as *mega grid* at ThedaCare. In reality, it is a decision matrix tool that allows the team to understand the *who* and *what* for each measure. The *who* is what payer or organization is seeking that information, and the *what* is the measure or quality outcome that is requested. There are a lot of other technical components to the analysts' work about what is needed to even begin measuring something, or to have the supporting pieces. Essentially, they determine *how* metrics are measured.

Once the analysts establish which metrics can be measured system wide, the quality department takes those to the department's senior leadership for feedback. After that feedback is incorporated, the quality metrics for True North developed by the department are taken to hospital senior leadership and the board. Once approved, the True North quality metrics will be disseminated. This is where the metrics start to come back full circle. The director and the coordinators will present the new metrics, what they measure, and why it matters for quality. They will have an open and interactive discussion about the new metrics and answer all questions patient-facing employees may have. The quality coordinators will then reinforce the new metrics by observation and coaching throughout the units. The quality department as a whole will monitor the progress on the metrics and provide coaching, resources, and support as needed so that the metrics can be made.

This example shows how the quality department helps understand the quality information, determine metrics that support True North, disseminate and teach patient-facing employees about metrics, and then support, teach, and review metric progress.

Positions and Responsibilities

Quality Coordinators

At ThedaCare, we use quality coordinators in a few different ways. There are two types of quality coordinators: ambulatory and hospital. A large part of both coordinators' role is to support employees, physicians, nurses, and so on, for specific quality requirements for specific patients. Coordinators help create a bridge between the quality department and care providers, which just means that they have direct contact with care providers more frequently. The quality department uses the crosswalk discussed in Chapter 2 to decide which initiatives will take priority. The coordinators are the channel that is most used to communicate standards and best practices. This may mean that new standards or best practices have been identified by another unit or another organization like the American Cancer Society, or the coordinators may be addressing a quality concern with a particular unit or floor that requires new or updated training to revisit standards and best practices. All coordinators are experienced nurses; this is key because the quality coordinators, although not directly involved in care delivery, will work with care delivery employees and must have enough experience to understand the work, the standards, and the industry best practices.

Coordinators are also key observers in ambulatory setting as well as in hospital care. It is crucial to catch quality issues before they escalate into larger problems—or hurt an employee or patient. Coordinators who are out on the floor in the units or clinics observing daily work catch quality issues early; they use concurrent chart audits to review and perform quality checks as the patient is in the hospital getting care. Thanks to work done by the data and business analysts, the coordinators can quickly see a quality concern and hopefully address the issue appropriately and prevent a larger problem from occurring. For instance, a clinic working on an improvement project may have overlooked tobacco cessation documentation in the electronic health record (EHR). The coordinators would be able to quickly identify this because the scorecards created by the business analysts would highlight that tobacco cessation documentation had decreased in the EHR. They could speak with the clinic and go observe the processes, and then the issue could be quickly resolved. Traditionally, this issue would not have been caught until the end of the month, or even every three months, depending on the reporting system.

In order to address an issue, an updated checklist may be distributed or a training event may be scheduled, it really depends on the scope of the issue observed. Although coordinators coach employees about standards and best practices and observed behaviors, they are not there daily to uphold those practices. Each practice or unit has administrators that oversee daily adherence to standards, and those administrators are supported by coordinators and updated on any changes to best practice.

For a concurrent chart review, quality coordinators would review the chart of a patient currently receiving care. For instance, a coordinator could notice that a patient had a urinary catheter by reviewing the cart; however, they notice that it has been more than 24 hours and there is no documentation to update whether or not the patient continues to need the catheter. The coordinator would then connect with the care team to find out if the patient needs the catheter, and if they do not, they will make sure the care team removes the catheter.

Concurrent chart reviews are an integral part of the work that inpatient quality coordinators do. This is a large reason why quality coordinators need a clinical background. Chart reviews require knowledge of care processes to understand what may or may not need to be completed, so they can identify when information is missing or if a test should be run. Coordinators also review and audit the Center for Disease Control's Vaccines for Children (VFC) Program. This program helps populations of children receive vaccines that might not get vaccines because of an inability to afford immunizations. The state's health departments provide the immunizations and oversee the program. Many families rely on the clinics to provide these VFC immunizations, so it is important that the program is run correctly and each clinic meets state requirements so that program funding is not taken away. Coordinators continuously review this program with standard work observations. The quality director goes to many of the clinics to observe as well as to stay current on the program and to serve as a resource and support employees administering the program.

Quality coordinators are all registered nurses, but they each have been at ThedaCare for many years. They also have the unique experience of working for the health plan that ThedaCare once owned and ran as care coordinators. Their knowledge and experience from the health plan is a valuable asset in understanding payer requirements and expectations. Coordinators should have clinical, leadership, and, if possible, care management experience. Key attributes for coordinators are strong communication skills and the ability to build teams and foster effective relationships.

Another component of coordinators' responsibilities also involves standards, and that is the Patient Care Review (PCR) team. The coordinators are part of a team that assesses missed opportunities—or complaints—that can be generated from nurses, doctors, patients, and even relatives of patients. The coordinators review the complaint or concern and the associated chart, and then create a summary of the issues to present to the PCR team; the team will then determine whether there is sufficient concern to warrant a full review and audit.

The major differences between ambulatory quality coordinators and hospital quality coordinators is that the latter work closely with data in EHR, CMS core measures, and concurrent chart review associated with core measures. The hospital measures are predominantly centered on acute care delivery and procedures, while the ambulatory coordinators have a much greater focus on preventive disease measure and health maintenance issues. Due to the knowledge base required and the level of teamwork needed between the coordinators and the care delivery teams, at ThedaCare it seems to work best to have two separate teams. At ThedaCare, the hospital quality coordinators spend a fair amount of time abstracting information from the EHR about core measures to submit to CMS. Once the EHR system is updated to incorporate that functionality, hospital quality coordinators will be able to spend more time coaching, observing and performing concurrent chart reviews. Hospital quality coordinators do real-time reviews of patient charts, again checking for core measures. This is done for two reasons: First, it is beneficial to have a second pair of eyes overseeing the quality of care for patients to ensure that processes are being followed and quality is ensured for the patient. The second reason is that concurrent reviews highlight patients that have care that is related to CMS core measures to ensure that the core measures are met for that patient. Retrospective chart review is helpful for identifying problem areas and training to prevent them, but by doing a concurrent review, the hospital quality coordinators can identify problems, address them, and train and adjust to prevent them in future while the patient is still being treated.

Business and Data Analysts

Quality can be viewed from many perspectives, but it is crucial for directors, managers, and coordinators to have accurate and accessible data that can be easily made into information that can support unit employee. We will not use the terms data and information interchangeably because they are not the same thing. Data refers to the raw information collected from patient surveys, the raw number of patients seen by a certain physician, in a clinic, or in a hospital and abstracted from the EHR. Information is what can be derived from data once it is analyzed. Information tells us what percentage of patients seen by a particular doctor have their required pneumonia vaccination called Pneumovax, and if that provider is improving toward the organizational target, or if they are more than two standard deviations from the group mean.

The crucial difference is that data are just raw numbers that need to be changed and made into actionable information, but you must first have data in order to attain information. Data collection is a double edge sword as too much info can paralyze, and on the other hand, a leader cannot skip data collection and hope to jump to the information phase where you can understand your current state. This does require a large level of data technical ability and system infrastructure. ThedaCare has had an electronic medical record (EMR) for 15 years, and they have leveraged that tool to collect data. They use patient surveys and Press Ganey to collect as much data about patient care, the care continuum, and outcomes as they can. The second part to this data and information picture is either having an in-house data analyst or an outside company who can turn the raw data into information with little lag time, if not in real time. These are two very large technological and technical investments that are absolutely required to bring the quality of care to the next level.

Business and data analysts are critical for ThedaCare and the entire quality department, because they create the reports, charts, and analysis that provide not just data but the information employees need to continue to provide quality care. They were very close together to make sure that the data sources are consistent and meet the needs of the patient-facing employees. Data analysts are mostly involved in the programming of the data; they work with the data structure and the processed data. They extract the data and transfer it for the business analysts to generate the reports. Data analysts look to create greater efficiencies in data collection and maintenance and for ways to further standardize data. Business analysts' primary role is to turn data into information; they will gather the requirements for the metrics. They work with the operational leaders to understand the business use for the data and then take the data from the data analyst and operationalize it into useful information. They assist the end users in understanding the data, and help guide them to answer their need. Business analysts help identify and call out gaps in processes from monitoring data sources. They generate reports or programs to help visualize the story from the data for the users. The business analyst is a *go between* for the business owners (operational leaders) and the technical side of the data abstraction and collection.

Employees depend on certain measures like infection rates or the number of patient falls to be in real time, but the goal is to eventually have all data in real time with no lag or gaps between information and the point at which the event occurred. Employees are better equipped to curb infection if they can be alerted as soon as the first or second peculiar infection is documented. Real-time data allows employees and improvement teams to be more responsive and, for quality concerns, to be dealt with more quickly. Some quality measures are looked at on a daily basis in each unit, some measures such as a fall or injury are looked at immediately, and the analysts are a vital part of getting and understanding this data. Before the data analysts' position was created, employee managers and directors were expected to analyze departmental data and report to their teams. The problem with this situation is that most employee managers are not trained nor do they have the data background needed to do that job, and it meant taking those leaders out of gemba and putting them behind a computer desk. Without full-time analysts, the managers, coordinators, and directors would spend substantially less time in gemba observing and coaching resulting in poor quality; hence, it becomes the quality department's responsibility to ensure that the important quality information is accurate and at their fingertips.

It is the responsibility of the business and data analysts to understand the criteria necessary for certain measures, the definition of each variable, such as the time of the day or day of the week that the patient was admitted that may influence outcomes. Data analysts know what inclusions and exclusions are necessary for reports such as the age parameters for measures; some measures only include those of age 18 and above and under the age of 65 years that have a specific list of health care condition codes, disease registry codes, or procedural codes. Variables are factors that could impact the outcome of a measure. This could mean age, race, sex, or other health conditions. These variables help the analyst understand variation. The quality analysts are also responsible for creating reports, charts, graphs for the quality department, and the leadership dashboards that are viewed daily. Another infrastructure or systems investment that had to be made at ThedaCare, in order for the data analyst to have quality data to work from, was to have standardized definitions for a fall, infection, medication error, and many others, so that a fall in the cardiac department means the same thing as a fall in the geriatric department or cancer department. This goes back to removing ambiguity from quality definitions and making the inclusion and exclusion criteria explicit. Everyone has to understand how they are included in a metric, or why they are not included in a metric.

The analysts know the data very well, because their job is to work with the data and create usable information from the info every single day. They dig deeper into the data, and ThedaCare pinpoints and finds where the targets and realities do not align, and digs down to a granular level to help determine the *why* behind the results; if they cannot determine the why based on current and even real-time data, they can report to managers to inform them that an issue exists and that a more detailed approach, such as an RCA, might be required.

The targets that the analysts keep their eyes out for are determined by the metric falling into one or more of the following categories (if applicable): 20 percent defect reduction, top one-third, or a statistically significant move in the metric (in the correct direction). You have to have trustworthy data and analysis, which requires high-quality data collection and a professional analyst. The organization must have, known and, defined variables, enough cases in the sample, and have reliable and testable results. Even in an organization like ThedaCare that is years into their lean journey, physicians will challenge the data and the information garnered from it—and that is not necessarily a bad thing. This means that the metrics and reports produced must be credible. Once you prove to physicians that this information is high quality and reliable *and* it is there to help them—not punish them—they will begin to accept this new method. In the end, the high standards of data and information help physicians perform, and the rigor that the physicians apply with their initial skepticism ultimately helps drive higher quality reports. All of these things benefit quality and, more importantly, the patient.

There are many requests for quality information and data from all over the organization, but the time of the analyst must be prioritized, and it is not efficient to duplicate work. Therefore, the director will sift through requests to determine which requests are high priority and will have the largest impact, but there is an expedited process for injuries or safety concerns. The director participates when needed or possible in rapid improvement events (RIEs)—an event that lasts a few days that includes employees, subject matter experts (SMEs), and sometimes pharmacists and patients to address a defect—and RCAs. RIEs are intense four-day long events where the RIE staff, generally at least one person from each part of the process that will be impacted, meet and develop an ideal state or target and then search for the root cause of the problem or issues that currently exist and develop an experiment or pilot to address the problem. Rapid implies that the changes are implemented now, in your work. RIEs are rewarding and can have a large impact, but they are intense with many moving parts and can be emotional for those involved. The director's involvement should help keep the event focused on the processes and questions to facilitate the group while they are developing an experimental solution. It is important to note that the role of the director in RIEs and RCAs is to support, observe, and ask questions to facilitate discussion; this model varies from organizations without lean where leaders and directors are often the people in charge and directing orders, rather than observing and facilitating while the employee leads the improvement work.

Quality Director

At ThedaCare, a quality director is a health care professional that has background and experience to understand the processes used in the delivery of care in the clinic or hospitals and to understand the patient flow, within a health care system. The skills or attributes for this role would include having strong communication skills, the ability to develop highly effective teams, and good personnel management skills. To work in a lean environment, the director really should have a theoretical and working knowledge of lean and six sigma. They should understand how to use the tools first hand as well as how to support employees and be a resource. A quality director must have a clinical background and have a master's degree in some health care area of health care or an MBA program. An additional skill that will help the director be successful is to be able to see and understand defects and waste.

This skill is valuable during gemba—observing the work where it is actually occurring. This role also requires someone with experience in management or leadership in addition to a clinical background in order to have developed their emotional intelligence and their ability to quickly build trust with individuals that they do not have previous relationships with. The quality directors are expected to work with payers—private and public. They must have an understanding of the interrelationship between health care delivery and the payment or incentive models for reimbursement by the payers; this knowledge and working relationship is required so that quality information can be provided to the divisional leaders to help them make resource and improvement decisions based off clinical quality gaps and payer payment models. This may mean ensuring that the required measures are reported to the correct entity, or understanding the risks of contracting with new or old payers and employers; the world of payers is often something that clinical professionals have little experience with, but as new payment reforms emerge, such as the Affordable Care Act, Meaningful Use, and private payer requirements, it is a large component of the quality director's work.

Although the payer component is large, the quality director mainly focuses on leading teams of people (coordinators, managers, analysts) and identifying, with other clinical leaders, what metrics are important to each division and patients. The quality director has a standardized calendar that includes the Patient Care Review Committee, Quality Oversight Committee, and the Quality Council meeting and other divisional leadership meetings. The directors will also have other areas of responsibility outside of the realm of clinical quality, which will also create calendar obligations. These committees and meetings are where discussions of larger issues, broader improvements, and general concerns can be discussed with divisional and senior-level leaders. The initiatives or gaps in quality discussed in these meetings have either been identified or the root cause at the unit level or a strategic initiative is now being delegated to a subcommittee for work. Through this process, we really try to support the bottom-up approach of lean, where the people closest to the work or the root cause of the problems can make the improvements to resolve the issues.

Data is a big component of quality at ThedaCare, and the quality director is part of the process for determining what metrics are important for the organization to track. This is a very important role for a data-driven organization; the goal is to track as many of the outcomes that will be helpful, but it takes resources and time to get the data collection structure built and work in the data collection into standardized work. To determine what metrics to invest resources into, the quality director and others will look at who is asking for the measures; for example, the metric could be how many diabetes patients have their cholesterol under control. CMS believes that not enough patients on Medicare are in control of their cholesterol, so they require control information to be submitted to them, and several private payers want that metric as they understand that maintaining an LDL to less than 100 is important as well in reducing patient risk of heart attacks and strokes. A metric that has three organizations that want it will likely be prioritized over other metrics that are only asked for by one or two organizations. To understand which organization or agency is asking for what measure, and the commonalities between the required measures, ThedaCare uses a crosswalk, pictured in Table 2.1. A crosswalk is really just a matrix where you can align things across two axes. The

Table 2.1 *The crosswalk used at ThedaCare to understand data needs and prioritize measures*

| Metric | Agency | | | | | Performance gap | Financial risk | Discrete data element |
	ACO	CMS	MU	Anthem	UHC	Y/N		
Hypertension	X	X		X	X	N	$	Y
Diabetes process bundle	X	X		X	X	Y	$	Y
Human papillomavirus (HPV)				X	X	Y	$	Y
Re-admissions	X	X	X	X		N	$	Y

crosswalk helps prioritize what measures will be added and monitored and to see which metrics would have the largest impact and meet the most requirements. In general, the director and other leaders try to look at all measures that *could* apply to an issue that organizations are wanting data on, and they try to make the best decision at the time while considering what future and possible government regulations they might require.

While we have identified some of the activities of the quality director, their biggest area of responsibility lies in improvement work. Value stream mapping helps gain a big picture idea of how a patient goes through the hospital from the first phone call to discharge. It can also help map out processes of employees. Simply stated, a value stream map is a visual representation of all the activities in a process from start to the end, for what is generally called a product family. The director helps create value stream maps, which are used to identify defects or waste for improvement at the unit level. For example, think of a patient that presents to the clinic for a routine physical. From the time that the patient walks in the door and is greeted by the registrar to the time the patient walks out the door with their new plan of care is an entire product family. Each step in that process, including making the appointment, insurance verification, health care questionnaire and paperwork, rooming, physician exam, ordering lab tests, and completion of the visit, is mapped to identify both value and nonvalue-added components.[6] Nonvalue-added components are those that do not improve value for the patient. Following the analysis of the current state value stream map, a future state is identified. Removing as much of the nonvalue-added process steps as possible, which may mean redesigning processes entirely, develops the future state. Nonvalue-added steps, which are plentiful, can be a patient waiting to be roomed, an employee going to get supplies, a patient being asked the same question multiple times by different people or on different forms, or duplicative steps in registration.

Figure 2.6 is a sample to demonstrate what is included in the value stream that starts at the supply line and goes through the steps in the process until the product makes it to the consumer. You first map the process as it is currently used, and then include all of the current steps. Then the team would look at the value stream and try to remove any unnecessary

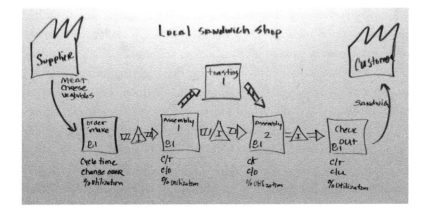

Figure 2.6 This is a value stream map that displays the core components that should be included when creating a value stream map with a process. It shows the start (supply line), the process steps (which can be more than four), and the output which is given to the customer

steps to streamline the process. A value stream map can be used for any process, for making a car, making a sandwich, or providing health care.

Department Role in Improvement

Supporting Improvement Work

The constant drive to improve processes and care delivery is what creates the momentum that keeps lean hospitals moving toward better and better care for patients. The quality department plays a large role in improvement work by supporting units and other leaders, identifying areas of improvement, and determining goals and targets. The department also monitors daily other measures like infection, and unit managers watch these indicators too, but the quality department monitors these measures and if a problem appears, they connect with the unit to see what is going on, if they have begun to address the issue, and if they need help or support. This is in contrast to the typical role of the quality department: monitoring all quality issues, determining solutions, implementing solutions, and owning all improvement work. The previous sentence uses the term *solution* broadly because in order for a countermeasure or a solution to work, it must address the root cause of the problem *and* be manageable by those who perform the tasks. This is difficult to accomplish in the traditional antiquated system of quality management. A countermeasure can be used as a stopgap solution to immediately alleviate or reduce the risk of harm until the true root cause can be identified and a solution be developed and put into place. Some defects can wait for a more developed plan, but defects that are related to safety should be addressed quickly in order to prevent harm.

At ThedaCare, the quality department makes an effort to *not* be the owner of improvement work. There are two reasons for this. First, as we alluded to before, it does not make sense for someone (the quality department) who does not do direct patient care or have patient interaction (seeing patients, admitting patients, laboratory testing) to be responsible for the changes made to improve the work. The quality department does not have to live with those changes daily or integrate the changes into their standardized work. It makes more sense to let the people who do the work every day to lead the improvement work and own the changes because they know what parts of the current system do and do not work; they know where improvements should be made. The quality managers do not know which supplies the nurses cannot find easily, where medical assistants have to create workarounds, or where the EMR does not allow communication between departments. Part of the improvement process is to study the implemented changes and adjust to further improve. This model is called PDSA, or plan, do, study, act. The employee that does that work every day and has observed new changes is best equipped to make adjustments and improve the process further.

The second is that having management, and in this case another department, step into a unit or clinic to manage their work without giving the workers ownership is *not* lean management. That is a traditional top-down model of management and it is an excellent way to make employees feel like they do not have control of their work and to decrease morale. Engaging employees and empowering them to improve their work and own their work will increase morale and improve employee satisfaction.

The quality department does strive to support and facilitate improvement work. This is accomplished by quality employees (managers, coordinators, and the director) getting involved in RCAs, RIEs, participating in gemba (where new ideas are brought forward and discussed), and seeking out and eliciting the expertise of SMEs when needed. The quality department is there to facilitate discussion and support patient-facing employees, so they can get to the best result; that may mean asking more questions to get to the root cause of an issue, or asking questions that get the employee to look at the problem differently, or providing relevant knowledge gained from improvement work done in another unit or clinic. Additional support may include training other employee members once the process has been improved. The role of the quality department in improvement work is to simply support the employee in the capacity that they need. The quality department also has the responsibility to keep their eyes on all of the other quality measures that are not the main focus of the divisional leadership teams and to raise the flag when a quality measure becomes an issue and alert the divisional leaders giving them an opportunity to act before the measure runs out of control.

Prioritizing Improvements

Once you know how to look for waste and defects, you will find them everywhere. This is both a good and a bad thing because the improvement opportunities are endless, but they can become overwhelming and difficult to sift through. Nurses, doctors, and others will see improvement opportunities everywhere, but the improvement work needs direction and coordination with department, division, and system strategic goals, or else it will become unmanageable and lack the needed resources to execute the improvement work. The quality department and patient-facing workers could find waste and improvement ideas anywhere they look, and if you asked any of them if they knew of any improvement ideas, they would have a long list of suggestions. The key to developing a strategic improvement initiative across a hospital or health care system is to focus improvement efforts on specific targets and goals. It is important to encourage employees to continue to identify problems while gently explaining why improvement ideas must be aligned with organizational goals or prioritized based on importance and impact. Leaders should keep employees engaged, and that engagement hinges on the employee trusting that leaders are listening and removing obstacles and focusing on the needs of the team.

The term *patient facing* is used instead of frontline to describe care team members who work with patients because frontline has a military connotation; its use suggests that those workers are at war with their patients, rather than partners in their care. At ThedaCare, the guiding principles of the organization are True North, which focuses on finance, quality and safety, the customer or patient, productivity, and employees. True North has an organization-wide set of goals; these goals are determined by senior leadership with the input of many employees and strategically deployed to each division. ThedaCare recognizes that the chief executive officer (CEO), chief financial officer (CFO), chief operating officer (COO), and vice president (VP) cannot move the metrics, but they can support the management and employees so that the goals can be met and provide resources for improvements.

At ThedaCare there is a corporate visual room that anyone can visit that has all of the True North metrics, goals, and even the number of employee injuries posted on the walls. These are not charts and jargon that only senior employees or analysts can understand; these are metrics that can be understood within five feet and five seconds. The North Wall holds all of the information the organization has decided is important for True North; this serves as their mission and vision wall. The South Wall holds all the run charts that are connected to other organizational strategies. The performance of those strategies is demonstrated by the run charts, which identifies the owner and shows performance trends and targets. The West Wall is True North performance; it contains each metric related to True North, the metric performance, the owner of the work, and what is currently being done to achieve the True North target. The West Wall is like the grounding wall; you know your mission and vision from the North Wall, but the West Wall puts it all in perspective and reminds the team of how the mission and vision will be achieved. The meeting rules are posted as well. The East Wall currently houses the work-wait board, which is where you see what work is being done and what work is currently on the back burner and needs to be done, or would be great to do.

Once the targets are set, they roll down to the divisional level managers. The divisional level leaders have their own visual room where they take the organization's goals and targets and break them down by services such as cancer or cardiovascular services. They look at how those groups can contribute to True North. Then the metrics are taken to the unit level; the targets are now specialized to metrics such as patient wait times, diabetes patient eye exams, or providing the pneumonia vaccine to at-risk patients. These goals at the unit level all contribute to the organizational goal of improving quality. The metrics are posted at the unit, divisional, and organizational level, and each metric has an owner—one person who is responsible for follow-up and where questions and ideas can be directed. Although the executive leadership sets the goals for the organization, it is only through the work at the unit level that the organizational metrics move. A real system of supportive engaged leaders is needed to have a coordinated system-wide improvement effort.

This system inevitably means that some improvement ideas are not addressed, but there is a system to choose which ideas to pursue. Keep in mind, however, many small improvements are made at the unit level every day that contribute to productivity that is owned by a unit member and monitored and followed through by unit members and leaders. In 2011, the cardiovascular unit at ThedaCare had a target of 220 unit improvements a year. That is the daily improvement organizations should strive to have, but some improvements require larger time commitments, labor hours, and unit collaboration or facilities involvement. When these improvement ideas are brought forward, they need to be assessed to ensure that they positively impact patient care and improve metrics for the unit, division, and the organization. Net promoter score, which is a customer loyalty and satisfaction index, and Press Ganey, are consulted when assessing an improvement idea to gain a clearer understanding of how the issue is affecting quality, patient care, and more. Safety issues are an exception to this process because they are assessed immediately so they can be addressed as soon as possible, since safety is an issue that can lead to direct patient or employee harm. The following figures are Pareto charts; these are used to break down data into manageable, digestible pieces. Pareto groups common themes and allows managers to visually see where the biggest group of problems exists. For example, this will show managers that infections after surgery have increased, and then by surgery, or building, or unit. This allows resources to be allocated in a way that targets the biggest issues at the source of the problem.

Once an idea is thoroughly examined and the data suggests that there are other areas that could have a larger impact for patients and would be less difficult to accomplish, the idea is taken to the PDSA level to develop a problem statement, goals, and target state. A tool used for the PDSA cycle is an A3, which is a problem solving tool that helps a team think through the current state, desired state, the gaps between those states, and countermeasures or actions to address those gaps. It is easy to know an improvement needs to occur, but it is helpful for the team to write down and define the problem and their desired outcome. Once those two are well established, the team can develop countermeasures to help achieve the desired state and put the ideas on paper. Then the idea would be taken to operations and oversights, which consists of the COO, chief marketing officer (CMO), and VPs, and they would review the idea and determine if it should be pursued, put on the hold, or kyboshed.

For large improvement that involves various parts of patient care, different units, admissions, and other aspects are difficult, near impossible to do without leadership support from the CEO down. However, units in organizations without a lean management system can still achieve great results and make improvements that impact their daily work and the patient. Start in one department and engage employees; once that unit's employees see that this process can improve their daily work, they will become more engaged and start asking for more and looking for new opportunities. Other departments will see improvements and start asking questions about what they did. When contemplating whether or not to start addressing process issues and to empower employees to become daily problem solvers, simply ask, "If not me, who? If not now, when?" It has to start somewhere, and lean is about applying a scientific method to quality improvement. So, you should start with a small pilot or experiment and then learn, adjust, and study it all over again. Once a unit starts showing results with better quality, improved budgets, less medicine reconciliation errors, or higher patient satisfaction, the unit can invite their managers and vice presidents to visit daily meetings to see the improvement and observe the changes. Change can start small, and starting small allows you to learn and adjust and then spread the improvements, but change must first start somewhere.

CHAPTER 3

Roof: True North, Sustainment Culture

Lean methodology is by no means the magic wand to improve quality in health care. An organization cannot expect their problems to be magically fixed after taking a few lean seminars, or doing a few rapid improvement events (RIEs) or root cause analyses (RCAs). Lean and other continuous improvement models provide the tools and methodologies that facilitate problem solving and critical thinking, but the tools are not enough to transform an organization.

The culture of the organization must be one of trust and empowerment so that employees are free to identify and solve problems without fear of shame and blame culture. An organization's culture is just a product of the experiences the employees, leaders, and even patients have while there, but that means that the culture is ultimately molded by the management system in place.[1] The culture will make or break a lean transformation. Without changing the culture, lean tools will only get an organization so far. Improvements can be made without cultural change, but employees will not be empowered and will lose motivation and energy to continue to fight for changes. Employees have to be supported and to feel valued, and that only happens with a cultural change. The culture component to lean allows employees to take pride in their work because *they* own it, and they are rewarded for their initiative. A cultural transformation requires the willingness to reassess job descriptions, roles, and responsibilities because as improvements take hold and old cultural practices are replaced, the function and role of each individual will inevitably change.[2]

The shame and blame culture ultimately prevents improvements from getting off the ground, and it limits the longevity of the improvement after they have been executed. When the culture of an organization is dysfunctional and at the most basic level, it prevents problems from being identified, addressed, and resolved, it also permeates the patient experience. If patient-facing workers feel unsupported, if they have low morale, or if they are frustrated by the problems they face and are unable to fix them, patients will notice them, and it will impact their perceptions and even their care. The patients and their families will observe this dysfunctional work environment and their experience of care will be impacted, their opinion of their provider will be impacted, and they may be afraid to bring forward concerns or issues after witnessing bickering colleagues, anger outbursts, or the lack of coordination among their team (Center for Advancing Health). The environment permeates all aspects of care that cannot be ignored if true transformation is the goal.

Although culture is critical to the success of lean, it can be a painful process to actually change it. Anyone who has ever tried to change a habit, such as nail biting or smoking, knows that it can be difficult to stop the undesired behavior, and even if you do change the behavior, it can be very easy to slip back into the old habit. David Mann differentiates between breaking and extinguishing habits. The same is true for the culture of a hospital—it is difficult to change, and once it has changed, it is easy to slip back into old cultural practices. Employees become accustomed to working around problems, not reporting them to management for fear of reprimand, or not working collaboratively to solve problems. Culture, experience, and behaviors are all interconnected. Culture builds and shapes behaviors, and behaviors shape experience (Figure 3.1).

The Bridges Transition Model is a great tool to use when planning organizational change. The model outlines three steps of transition.[3] The first is a fear of the unknown, denial, anger, and a sense of loss. It is important to remember and acknowledge that the forthcoming changes could mean that people who have been co-workers for many years may be separated by new facilities. Or, unit upgrades and renovations may mean that the employees who have worked there for 20 years may be losing the facility that feels like home. The second step is resentment, low morale, and anxiety. Resentment may be targeted at higher-up leaders or it may be targeted at direct supervisors or even co-workers. It is important to recognize where these feelings are coming from and to coach and support employees through them. The third step in the model is high energy, open learning, and renewal of commitment that come with the beginning of a

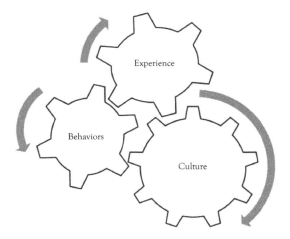

Figure 3.1 An illustration of how experiences drive behaviors and create a culture

new chapter or opening of a new building. Employees will be excited and eager but only after they have moved through steps one and two. Each employee member will move through the model at a different pace. One team member may already be in step three when another member is only in step one. The leader's job during transition is to identify those who are having trouble moving through the transition and give them the support, comfort, and training they need to be able to progress.[4]

Change impacts leaders as well. Leaders will move through the transition model just like employee members, and they must be acutely aware of their feelings and attitudes. A leader with anger, resentment, or low morale can inadvertently instill fear in their team, act resentful for them, or miss important coaching and support opportunities.

Employees will, like all humans, want to resort back to what is comfortable. They will want to do what they know and feel comfortable doing. The role of leadership is to step in and make the transition more comfortable and to coach and support employees through changes. David Mann calls this cultural inertia, which means that to maintain improvements there must be a management process, like coaching and observing, to support the changes. Managers should be on the floor—not in their office—so they can support employees, ease fears, and smooth the transition. Managers can observe and coach employees to new standards and help keep people from sliding back into their comfortable old habits. Coaching in this example does not mean telling employees they are wrong; it means asking them how they can help them do their job better. What is keeping them from doing an even better job each day? Are there problems with the new standards?

Do be warned, management presence is a double-edged sword. It is necessary to help support changes, but it can also be perceived by employees as management hovering, watching over their shoulder, micromanaging, snooping, and being aggressive. Their feelings are not wrong and should not be disregarded. If managers just hover over the shoulders of others, point out mistakes, and tell people how they can do their job better, it will not go over well. That is not a successful way to change an organization. The change has to start with leadership. If managers are not supportive, engaged, co-operative, actively listening, and more, the employees will view their presence negatively. Do note that some employees will view their presence negatively regardless of how the manager behaves and supports employees. Hospitals may lose employees who are unwilling to change, and that is to be expected. Change is hard on everyone, and we want it to be clear that this is not a painless process. The quality rewards of transformation, though, can be incredible. The results that can be achieved through a lean transformation can increase patient and employee satisfaction, as well as care outcomes.

Building Emotional Capital

The need to prepare employees for change cannot be stressed enough. We often hear about building human capital with training, education, and conferences, but we rarely hear about building employees' emotional capital. As we said earlier, going through organizational changes will create tension, there will be rough patches, and your employees will be faced with new and uncomfortable routines. It is important to build their *emotional bank*, so to speak, because as leaders we will be withdrawing on their emotional bank as we work through the changes in the improvements. It is important that leaders recognize the emotional impact that changes can have on employees. Managers need to provide positive feedback and support prior to any changes so employees have a repository of positive, supportive, and encouraging thoughts to pull from during difficult times. This requires planning. The organization must plan changes thoroughly and give managers enough time to prepare workers for changes and their emotional capital. Assessments can be completed to determine a team's readiness to undertake large changes. The readiness assessment can provide affirmation that the team is ready to take on large projects and let readers know what previous work the team has done, which will prepare the area or team for substantial changes that often accompany improvement work.

The readiness assessment looks at how large and complex the value stream is, other stakeholders that are involved in this value stream that might be impacted by changes, leadership structure and length of time the leadership structure has been in place, system structure, and system and personnel barriers. There is no quantitative way to assess this information. The best one can do is observe the processes and for people to see each of these categories in motion, as well as talk to employees and leadership to understand their acceptance level.

This may sound strange to some, but the concept of building up or stockpiling positive emotions and experiences is not a new concept. James C. Hunter describes building the emotional bank of employees; basically, Hunter argues that large organizational changes will take from employee's emotional banks.[5] You have to deposit positive, truthful, and encouraging support into employee's emotional banks prior to changes, or else they may be pulling from an empty bank. The withdrawal made during transition will always be larger than a singular deposit;[6] to compensate for this, there should be plenty of planning time allotted so that leaders can work with and develop their team and prepare them for the transition by building their emotional bank.

Employees may not even know how stressful the change is until it is over, but these vast changes can keep people late at work, will work on their minds even while they are at home, and can overall impact them on an emotional level. It is important to remember that everyone is human, which means everyone has emotions that should be acknowledged. Managers must lessen the stress by allowing employees to verbalize their feelings and let their feelings be heard by compassionate ears. This is where leaders' emotional intelligence needs to be strong. Employees will verbalize their feelings of fear, frustration, and whatever else is impacting them, and leaders must know that employees are not personally attacking them, but instead they are dealing with the change process and verbalizing how it is impacting them. Leaders must also remember that employees will be going through different stages of change at different times. It is the role of the leader to recognize this difference and to celebrate the good and when an improvement ends so that employees can take a moment to celebrate the end of a project and get closure. Senior leaders should observe interactions between employees and use those opportunities to coach leaders to improve their emotional intelligence. This is just another example of how the inverted pyramid, where the senior leadership is on the bottom, supporting employees, is executed.

According to Bridges Transitional Model, employees will go through three stages: (1) ending, losing, and letting go; (2) the neutral zone; and (3) the new beginning.[7] This list is slightly misleading because it makes the process of dealing with change appear uniform, which is not the case. Each employee will progress through these stages at a different rate. It is the role of the manager to get all employees to accept and integrate. It is the manager's responsibility to ask employees how they can be supported better, what obstacles are in their way, and how to help them. Lean leadership never stops being a critical component to quality. Lean leadership and lean culture are the glue that keep the organization functioning in this improvement model. It is a delicate balance to not swing too far in the process direction, because it can mean that emotions can be overlooked. It is an important lesson to not become consumed with the process and the expense of people.

At ThedaCare the changes started small; the goal initially was to prove to physicians that this was not a leadership gimmick and to improve the things that mattered to them. A simple RCA soon led a team to request to completely overhaul their Medical Services unit—the new unit would use a collaborative care model with a pharmacist, nurse manager, and physician, developing a care plan at the patient's bedside. This improvement, however, did not happen overnight and required an extraordinary amount of time and dedication from the team that created and tested the model. Ultimately, collaborative care was an enormous success and continues to provide outstanding quality of care, but it was a draining (and rewarding) task for those involved.

The Daily Continuous Struggle

The title of this subsection is a play on the lean term daily continuous improvement; however, you and your employee will have daily struggles—big and small—to sustain improvements. The struggle will vary in intensity, but it will always exist. The more improvements that are undertaken and implemented, the harder it will be to sustain your past improvements. It is very similar to studying for classes; as you pay more attention on one subject, others will suffer if you do not manage your time efficiently. The same concept is true for improvement work. As resources are diverted to new improvements, the previous improvements could suffer. This is where many organizations may begin to tread water or plateau, but if there is a continuous daily improvement (CDI) system, then support system organizations can make great strides. The sustainment of previous improvement efforts can keep the organization moving forward at a steady incline, but if organizations make an improvement and stall, it is more like they make improvements step by step—like a staircase. It is easy for everyone to be excited and enthusiastic during the improvement process, but it is hard to maintain that enthusiasm and the energy needed to maintain those improvements two months, six months, and years after the initial improvement.

In theory, CDI seems simple to define: Working daily to solve problems and improve workflow, efficiency, safety, and quality. But in reality, it is more difficult to define the real expectations of individual employees and the scope of CDI. ThedaCare still struggles to define the scope of CDI. The original ideal state was to have leaders walk their teams through daily problem solving, but that has not worked out as it was intended. It is taking more time out of everyone's day and the work is not delivering as much in quality terms. It has been observed that there is far more *bang for the buck* or more measurable improvement from identifying when there is a need for a standard either because one does not exist or the standard was not being adhered to (and looking at the reasons *why* the standard was not used). It is easy to do kaizen after kaizen and have big sexy RIEs; however, that method will contribute to the daily struggle to sustain quality improvement. All of those improvement events do not necessarily feed into the value stream progression. Your organization will be running in place, and, eventually, it will impact the morale of your employees. Organizations will look back and see that, while kaizen events were happening, none of the new improvements were actually sustained, and the goals had not been achieved. That result will build frustration and confusion in employees. It will be difficult, and there is not a one size fits all answer to how to define the scope of CDI, but an organization must be cognizant that CDI needs limitations and structure.

Value stream maps are an important concept for a lean organization, but they are even more important for a targeted quality improvement approach. This map helps everyone understand what the priorities of the organization are and how measures, progress, improvements, and standardized work fit into the value stream. It is a visual way to see the entirety of a process and understand each step, large and small. Value stream maps make employees think about the little steps that often get overlooked or taken for granted. It also helps identify wasteful steps in the process. Your current state includes every step in the current process so that the team can identify wasteful parts in the process to remove for the future state value stream map.

A classic trap that organizations can fall into is doing kaizen after kaizen after kaizen. That is simply exhausting. Kaizens are events that span multiple days, and that means those involved are not doing their usual daily work. It means that there will be a tremendous amount of new improvements, standards, and outcomes to track, which will rapidly overwhelm your units and management. Something will have to give and one or more of the improvements will revert to old standards or habits, which means meaningful progress is lost and will require rework. Do not fall into this kaizen trap. Do not set goals or targets for completing multiple kaizens. ThedaCare made this mistake initially and made quotas for kaizens. Improvements are more important than the number of kaizens. Your organization should pick quality issues such as infection or patient satisfaction and then use those goals as a starting point for improvement work. The rapid kaizen path is one filled with exhausted employees and weakened morale, because they will overexert themselves and their hard work will not be sustained.

The key to preventing a plateau from taking place is to acknowledge that you, according to David Mann, "are the force that can motivate and sustain the lean management in your units." This statement is true for the CEO, VPs, managers, and patient-facing employees. You will have to work daily to support employees and maintain improvements, and your employees will also have to work continuously to sustain the departmental improvements. Quality is not sustained by implementing changes and then expecting them to just work or sustain them. Managerial support *on the floor* has to be a priority because otherwise the resources that were used to make the initial improvement were, in a sense, wasted, because new resources will have to be allocated to do rework. The overarching goal of a lean management system for quality is to create no defects and to pass along no defects, and waste is most certainly a defect. Quality was defined earlier as zero defects accepted, created, or passed on. If your processes slip back to preimprovement standards that allow the defects to *reenter* the process, with the potential to be passed onto others, then the department has to rework to fix the process a second time.

Another key is understanding that your organization does not have the answers to every problem, or that someone else may have already come up with an answer that will work for you as well. Networks such as the ThedaCare Center for Health Care Value's Healthcare Value Network (HVN) and Clinical Business Intelligence Network (CBIN) allow leaders from all over the United States and the world to connect, learn, and share.[8] The HVN is for health care systems that are at a certain point of development in their lean transformation to come together through an interactive user website, an annual summit, and through planned gemba visits to member organizations. Gemba visits are usually multiple days at a network member site where 10 to 20 attendees are afforded the opportunity to go and see what work is being done, how they are doing it, ask questions, share materials, and connect with others who are working on similar issues or may serve as a content expert or resource. The network members acknowledge that no one organization has all of the answers and that a collaborative environment benefits them all, but all members are far enough geographically where they are not competitors. CBIN is a newer network developed to address the growing need for real-time analytics, data infrastructure, and integration into daily work. Other industries are far ahead of health care in that respect, but with the help of Gartner(r), the network is working to close that gap and develop best practices. The networks have different focuses, but their goal is the same: create an environment where health care leaders can learn and share best practices, experiments, and even failures with one another, so they can all work to provide the highest quality of care and the highest value for the patient.

CHAPTER 4

Conclusion

A quality management strategy for an organization that is seeking to or has already implemented a continuous improvement program must include respect for people, a transparent and open culture, employee empowerment, and actively engaged leaders. These are the elements that build an organization that values people, and when an organization puts the highest value on people, then quality efforts can focus on improving outcomes for people. There are more tangible and measurable components and tools that accompany a lean quality management system, such as root cause analyses, improvement slips, checklists, and observations. What cannot be stressed enough is that to unlock high-quality health care outcomes for patients and for employees, you must have both the supportive and transparent culture with the more traditional tools and measures. Organizations must also realize that the customer determines quality, regardless of the environment. We all have a standard that we measure each consumer exchange by whether that exchange is at a local coffee shop or the hospital. In order to achieve high-quality outcomes, organizations must recognize the voice of the customer.

Change has to start somewhere, and, sometimes, you just have to make the case for change, which could mean starting out extremely small in your own department to convincing management to adopt new practices. With those changes, small or large, the caliber of the data collection must be set as high as your organizational capacity will allow. Without accurate, complete, and high-quality data, performance cannot be assessed prior to or after improvements are implemented, and if you cannot assess performance before you make changes, there is no way that you or the employee can be sure that the proposed changes will really positively impact the targeted problem. You will also need trained employees who can analyze data for your organization. Employee training is crucial for all aspects of a lean transformation whether your focus is on quality or something else—although we do question how one could adopt lean if quality was not the focus.

It will be unsurprising to any person who has worked in health care that it is complicated, and making changes can be arduous. We do not want to underplay the amount of work, time, and thought that will be required to transform and manage quality in a lean organization, but we do want to provide a better blueprint for those who are frustrating and yearning for improvement, those who have started and need guidance, or anybody else that desires to learn about managing and improving health care, quality. Systems will need to be created, trainings completed, relationships built, and more, but if you are committed to high-quality health care you must commit to all aspects of continuous improvement, and sometimes they are not glamorous.

Checklist for Continued Quality

- Go and see. Go visit other health care organizations in your region who are high performing lean organizations, or go visit a manufacturer who is using lean and observe, learn, and ask questions.
- Get yourself and your organization a coach, mentor, or consultant. Lean is for the long haul and you will need support, and so will your organization.
- Develop or adopt a management system to help you sustain your improvements and provide stability and standardization.
- Use your data to drive results, which means having an informatics team and understanding your financial, quality, and other drivers.
- Continue to build and reinforce a culture of transparency with data, results, and qualities within your organization.
- Read and learn from others. Suggested reading list:
  - *On the Mend*
  - *Everything I Know About Lean I Learned in First Grade*
  - *Perfecting Patient Journeys*

APPENDIX 1

RCA Standard Work

Root Cause Analysis (RCA) Event

Last Updated	XX/XX/XX	Owner		Performed By		Work	N/A
Takt Time	N/A	Revised By		Rev. Number	6	In	
		Trigger	RCA prep complete	Done		Process	

PDSA is documented and communicated to all appropriate Leadership groups.

Standard Work

#	Major Steps	Details (if applicable)	Time
1	RCA Leader sets up the room.	Post the following in the room in this order: • Agenda • RCA Purpose • Team Rules • Problem Statement • Timeline (include trigger and done) • Top Contributors – Impact • Root Cause – 5 Why • Top Contributors/Root Cause/Countermeasures • Summary • Action Plan • Communication Plan • Parking Lot	30 min
2	RCA Leader kicks off the team.	Introductions, RCA purpose, housekeeping, agenda overview, team rules.	5 min
3	RCA leader reviews the brief context of the incident, problem statement and scope of RCA with the team.	Validate and update the problem statement with input from the team.	10 min
4	Take the team to gemba.	Take the team to the actual place where the problem/near miss/sentinel event occurred. Share any relevant evidence from the specific event (equipment, location, etc...).	20 min

Diagram, Work Flow, Picture, Time Grid

Tip · Tollgate · WIP · Critical Step · Team Safety

RCA Purpose: Understand the underlying reason(s) the problem happened in order to prevent it from happening again. It is not intended to place blame on a person but rather to look for defects in the process.

Agenda:
Kick off
Problem Statement
Gemba Walk
Time Line
Potential Contributors
Roots Causes
Potential Countermeasures
Action Plan
Communication Plan

Problem Statement: Include **what** happened, **who** is involved or impacted, **where** the problem occurred, **when** the problem occurred **how** the problem occurred (method), **how often/how many** times and what are the **consequences.**

Time Line

Trigger	When Who What	When Who What	When Who What	Done

Root Cause Analysis (RCA) Event

Last Updated	XX/XX/XX	Owner	Performed By	All	Work In	N/A
Takt Time	N/A	Revised By	Rev. Number	6	Process	
		Trigger	Done	PDSA is documented and communicated to all appropriate Leadership groups.		

RCA prep complete

Standard Work

#	Major Steps	Details (if applicable)	Time	Diagram, Work Flow, Picture, Time Grid
5	RCA Leader reviews the timeline/process flow.	Validate and update the timeline/process flow with input from the team. 😊 Tip: Use the right brain/left brain exercise to identify team members thoughts at each of the process steps see [drive location] Ask each team member who was present during the event to silently complete the right brain/left brain exercise on the document. Ask each member to debrief with the team on what they wrote on the document and write down "what they said" on a pink post it and "what they were thinking" on a purple post it . Place the "What was said" and the "What I was Thinking" post its under the appropriate process steps.	30 min	
6	RCA Leader asks the team to identify points in the timeline/process flow where potential contributions to the problem occurred.	Keep the team focused on issues that contributed to the problem statement, not just any general process problems. 😊 Tip: Use a different color post-it to differentiate from the time line. Ask team to reflect on what was said and what they were thinking. Did this contribute to the problem?	30 min	
7	Summarize and prioritize the top 3 – 5 contributors to the problem.	Consolidate similar "problem contributors" to avoid redundancy. Determine which contributors have the greatest impact to the problem statement. If we eliminate this contributor, will this prevent similar incidents from occurring?	10 min	
8	Break	Conduct energy break	10	
9	Identify the root causes to the top contributors.	Use 5 whys to understand the root causes. 😊 Tip: Use a different color post-it to differentiate from the time line and potential contributors.	45 min	

Trigger

When Who What   When Who What   When Who What

When Who What   When Who What

Done

Problem	Root Cause	Countermeasure

Root Cause Analysis (RCA) Event

Last Updated	XX/XX/XX	Owner		Performed By	All		Work In	N/A
		Revised By		Rev. Number	6		Process	
Takt Time	N/A	Trigger	RCA prep complete	Done	PDSA is documented and communicated to all appropriate Leadership groups.			

Standard Work

	Major Steps	Details (if applicable)	Time	Diagram, Work Flow, Picture, Time Grid
10	Verify the root causes.	All root causes should be verified or proved. To ensure that the root cause addresses the main problem track back each "why" from the root cause up to the main problem. Example: If we do this, then this will be fixed, which will fix our main problem!	10 min	
11	Develop potential countermeasures to each root cause.	Use the appropriate style of brainstorming that will work with your team (silent, group, 7 ways, etc . . .) 😊 Tip: Use a different color post-it to differentiate from the time line, potential contributors and root causes.	30 min	
12	Create an action plan.	Identify details behind each action item: What is the action, Who will be performing the action, When will it be completed by.	15 min	
13	Create a communication plan.	Identify who needs to be communicated with in order for the action plan to be effective. Document detail behind each communication item: What needs to be communicated, To Whom will it be communicated to, Who will be performing the communication, When will it be communicated.	10 min	
14	Determine metrics to study if countermeasures are effective.	Ask the team to identify what will be measured, who will be measuring it, the frequency and duration .	10 min	
15	Document on PDSA template.	Follow PDSA standard work to document the PDSA focus ing on the facts and using roles not names of people (patient, RN, Provider etc.) 😊 Tip: Document the timeline in the "background/ current conditions ", the action plan in the "do" , the metrics and study plan in the "study" section of the PDSA. Schedule appropriate follow-up to complete study and act portions of the PDSA.	60 min	

What	Who	When

Root Cause Analysis (RCA) Event

Last Updated	XX/XX/XX	Owner		Performed By	All	Work	N/A
		Revised By		Rev. Number	6	In	
Takt Time	N/A	Trigger	RCA prep complete	Done	PDSA is documented and communicated to all appropriate Leadership groups.	Process	

Standard Work

	Major Steps	Details (if applicable)	Time	Diagram, Work Flow, Picture, Time Grid
16	Communicate PDSA with all appropriate Leadership groups including your one up.	Send sentinel event, patient harm and all other patient related PDSAs to the Quality Manager or representative.		
		Create a spread plan where appropriate.		
		Send staff harm to OSHA team lead.		

Root Cause Analysis (RCA) Event

Last Updated	XX/XX/XX	Owner		Performed By	All		Work	N/A
		Revised By		Rev. Number	6		In	
Takt Time	N/A	Trigger		Done			Process	

RCA prep complete   PDSA is documented and communicated to all appropriate Leadership groups.

Job Instruction Sheet

⊙ Tip ◆ Tollgate ⊘ WIP ▽ Critical Step ✚ Team Safety

	Major Steps	Details (if applicable)	Reasons (Why)
1	RCA Leader sets up the room.	Post the following in the room in this order: • Agenda • RCA Purpose • Team Rules • Problem Statement • Timeline (include trigger and done) • Top Contributors - Impact • Root Cause – 5 Why • Top Contributors/Root Cause/Countermeasures Summary • Action Plan • Communication Plan • Parking Lot	So all involved can see the problem as clearly as possible.
2	RCA Leader kicks off the team.	Introductions, RCA purpose, housekeeping, agenda overview, team rules.	Ensures everyone understands the purpose of the RCA process. 1) What happened? 2) Why did it happen? 3) What can be done to prevent or reduce the likelihood of a reoccurrence?
3	RCA leader reviews the brief context of the incident, problem statement and scope of RCA with the team.	Validate and update the problem statement with input from the team.	This statement will help remind you of what things are in or out of scope and why you started down this path. The problem statement is very important in order to communicate what you are working on and why.
4	Take the team to gemba.	Take the team to the actual place where the problem/near miss/sentinel event occurred. Share any relevant evidence from the specific event (equipment, location, etc...).	Gemba is the first place to look to understand a problem. This gives the team the opportunity to see the environment surrounding the process and ask clarifying questions.

Root Cause Analysis (RCA) Event

Last Updated	XX/XX/XX	Owner	Performed By	All	Work	N/A
Takt Time	N/A	Revised By / Trigger	Rev. Number	6	In Process	
		RCA prep complete	Done	PDSA is documented and communicated to all appropriate Leadership groups.		

Job Instruction Sheet

◕ Tip ◆ Tollgate ⊙ WIP ▽ Critical Step ✚ Team Safety

	Major Steps	Details (if applicable)	Reasons (Why)
5	RCA Leader reviews the timeline/process flow.	Validate and update the timeline/process flow with input from the team. ◕ Tip: Use the right brain/left brain exercise to identify team members thoughts at each of the process steps see O:\ThedaCare_Improvement_System\+Friday Report Outs\Report Out A3\LEFT-RIGHT BRAIN FUNCTIONS.docx Ask each team member who was present during the event to silently complete the right brain/left brain exercise on the document. Ask each member to debrief with the team on what they wrote down and write down "what they said" on a purple post it and "what they were thinking" on a pink post it . Place the "What was said" and the "What I was Thinking" post its under the appropriate process steps.	This allows the team to apply their eyes on the timeline to add relevant information that may have been missed. The timeline indicates "what" occurred. However, participants may have had thoughts at the time that may also help to identify problems. For example, was their confusion, was another action considered, etc.
6	RCA Leader asks the team to identify points in the timeline/process flow where potential contributions to the problem occurred.	Keep the team focused on issues that contributed to the problem statement, not just any general process problems. ◕ Tip: Use a different color post-it to differentiate from the time line. Ask team to reflect on what was said and what they were thinking. Did this contribute to the problem?	This will lead the team towards the main contributors and their root causes.
7	Summarize and prioritize the top 3 – 5 contributors to the problem.	Consolidate similar "problem contributors" to avoid redundancy. Determine which contributors have the greatest impact to the problem statement. If we eliminate this contributor, will this prevent similar incidents from occurring?	By concentrating on the main contributors it allows the team to focus. In many cases many of the main contributors have the same root cause.
8	Break	Conduct energy break	Allows everyone a physical and mental break from the process.

Root Cause Analysis (RCA) Event

Last Updated	XX/XX/XX	Owner		Performed By	All		Work	N/A
Takt Time	N/A	Trigger		Rev. Number	6		In	Process
			RCA prep complete	Done				

PDSA is documented and communicated to all appropriate Leadership groups.

Job Instruction Sheet

😊 Tip ◆ Tollgate ⊗ WIP ▽ Critical Step ✚ Team Safety

	Major Steps	Details (if applicable)	Reasons (Why)
9	Identify the root causes to the top contributors.	Use 5 whys to understand the root causes. 😊 Tip: Use a different color post-it to differentiate from the time line and potential contributors.	To address the root cause rather than a symptom.
10	Verify the root causes.	All root causes should be verified or proved. To ensure that the root cause addresses the main problem track back each "why" from the root cause up to the main problem. Example: If we do this, then this will be fixed, which will fix this, which will fix our main problem!	By following through the 5 why process it builds quality into whatever solution is brainstormed.
11	Develop potential countermeasures to each root cause.	Use the appropriate style of brainstorming that will work with your team (silent, group, 7 ways, etc . . .) 😊 Tip: Use a different color post-it to differentiate from the time line, potential contributors and root causes.	In order to get as many potential countermeasures to address the root causes.
12	Create an action plan.	Identify details behind each action item: **What** is the action, **Who** will be performing the action, **When** will it be completed by.	In order to assign responsibility for ensuring follow through for the RCA.
13	Create a communication plan.	Identify who needs to be communicated with in order for the action plan to be effective. Document detail behind each communication item: **What** needs to be communicated, **To Whom** will it be communicated to, **Who** will be performing the communication, **When** will it be communicated.	To ensure all who need awareness of this issue has the appropriate communication to prevent recurrence and increase confidence for all involved.
14	Determine metrics to study if countermeasures are effective.	Ask the team to identify **what** will be measured, **who** will be measuring it, the **frequency** and **duration**.	We always want to use data to determine if our countermeasures are effective as we study and act.

Root Cause Analysis (RCA) Event

Last Updated	XX/XX/XX	Owner		Performed By	All		Work	N/A
Takt Time	N/A	Revised By		Rev. Number	6		In	
		Trigger	RCA prep complete	Done			Process	

PDSA is documented and communicated to all appropriate Leadership groups.

Job Instruction Sheet

⊙ Tip ◆ Tollgate ⊙ WIP ▽ Critical Step ✚ Team Safety

	Major Steps	Details (if applicable)	Reasons (Why)
15	Document on PDSA template.	Follow PDSA standard work to document the PDSA focusing on the **facts and using roles not names of people (patient, RN, Provider etc.)** ⊙ **Tip:** Document the timeline in the "**background/current conditions**", the action plan in the "**do**", the metrics and study plan in the "**study**" section of the PDSA. Schedule appropriate follow-up to complete study and act portions of the PDSA.	We always want to use PDSA thinking when solving a problem. Documenting the thought process on a PDSA template helps others to visually see the story behind understanding and solving the problem.
16	Communicate PDSA with all appropriate Leadership groups including your one up.	Send sentinel event, patient harm and all other patient related PDSAs to the Quality Manager or representative. Create a spread plan where appropriate. Send staff harm to OSHA team lead.	Quality Manager or representative and OSHA team leads will track and trend RCA work to identify system issues.

Root Cause Analysis (RCA) Event

Last Updated	XX/XX/XX	Owner		Performed By	All	Work In Process	N/A
	N/A	Revised By		Rev. Number	6		
Takt Time		Trigger	RCA prep complete	Done	PDSA is documented and communicated to all appropriate Leadership groups.		

Process Owner Overview

	Major Steps	Work Time	Wait Time	Process Observations
1	RCA Leader sets up the room.			
2	RCA Leader kicks off the team.			
3	RCA leader reviews the brief context of the incident, problem statement and scope of RCA with the team.			
4	Take the team to gemba.			
5	RCA Leader reviews the timeline/process flow.			
6	RCA Leader asks the team to identify points in the timeline/process flow where potential contributions to the problem occurred.			
7	Summarize and prioritize the top 3 – 5 contributors to the problem.			
8	Break			
9	Identify the root causes to the top contributors.			
10	Verify the root causes.			
11	Develop potential countermeasures to each root cause.			
12	Create an action plan.			
13	Create a communication plan.			
14	Determine metrics to study if countermeasures are effective.			
15	Document on PDSA template.			
16	Communicate PDSA with all appropriate Leadership groups including your one up.			

Diagram, Work Flow, Picture, Time Grid

Tip ◆ Tollgate ⊗ WIP ▽ Critical Step ✚ Team Safety

APPENDIX 2

Huddle Board Standard Work

What Do the People Look Like?

- Staff are ready to go, may even arrive before leader and self-start if the leader is not there
- Eye contact with each other
- Everyone contributes
- Everyone around board
- Standard work referenced and in hand
- No dominance or intimidation
- Staff rather than leaders do most of the talking
- Leader ready and removes obstacles
- Laughter, smiling, eagerness
- Leader is coaching and engaging everyone
- Everyone is focused—no side conversations
- Focus, expedience, pride, passion all exhibited

What Do You Hear?

- Barriers identified
- Problems, ideas, possible solutions
- Is there standard work?
- Volunteers
- Deadlines
- What are the next steps?
- Creativity
- Laughter and fun
- Stop the complainers

- Pull for other departments
- Asking for help
- Empathy and interest
- Staff doing more talking than leaders
- Concern and compassion for patients
- Delegation
- Connections to drivers, and so on
- Discussion about just do it versus plan, do, study, act (PDSA)
- Staff recognizes PDSA thinking
- Clarification
- Honesty
- Discussion about capacity
- Recognition and cooperation
- Discussion about safety
- Links to other projects
- Respect and candor

What Do the Boards Look Like?

- Standard
- See status *at a glance*
- Variety in owners
- Reflects current completion dates and information
- Be realistic about quantity of improvements *in process*
- Lanes balanced around triangle
- Opportunities linked to drivers
- Change observed in movement of work
- Needs to be actionable not informational

APPENDIX 3

PICK Chart Standard Work

PICK Chart

Last Updated	XX/XX/XX	Owner		Performed By	Everyone	Work In	1
		Revised By		Rev. Number	3	Process	
Takt Time	NA	Trigger	Need to identify solutions	Done	Solutions ranked		

Standard Work

	Major Steps	Details (if applicable)	Time	Diagram, Work Flow, Picture, Time Grid
	Brainstorm Solutions			
1	Take top root causes identified in Gap Analysis and place vertical order on flip chart.		2 min	
2	Ask team to brainstorm potential solution for identified problem, one at a time. Tips: At least 3 solutions for each root cause. Tell them there are no dumb ideas and NO DISCUSSION! (Don't let the team get wrapped up in if the solution will work or not, just keep throwing out ideas) Could be done as silent brainstorm to get all ideas on table.	Silent brainstorm can be done by having everybody write ideas on post-its and then giving them to the facilitator, instead of going around the room to have team members say ideas out loud	5 min per problem	
3	List all potential solutions opposite of identified problem and review with team		10 min	
	Prioritize Solutions			
4	Prioritize solutions based on impact to metrics. Create a PICK Chart using 3M paper like the example. You will want to place each solution onto the PICK chart one at a time getting feedback from the team as to if it's High or Low Impact and then Low or High Difficulty	Impact should be based on Impact to Metrics	1 hr	
1 5	Each solution will then fall into the categories of Possible, Implement, Challenge and Kill (spelling PICK)			
2 6	Use highest rated solutions for trials TIP: You will likely want to focus the group on the items in Implement area first. This helps the group focus on certain solutions before others.	• Focus on the Implement area first. • Don't even consider items in the Kill area. If an idea has low impact and is difficult to implement, there is no need to work on it	15 min	

Tip   Tollgate   WIP   Critical Step   Team Safety

Impact — HIGH / LOW   Difficulty — HIGH

Implement / Kill / Possible / Challenge

PICK Chart

Last Updated XX/XX/XX	Owner		Performed By Everyone	Work In 1
	Revised By		Rev. Number 3	Process
Takt Time NA	Trigger	Need to identify solutions	Solutions ranked Done	

😊 Tip ◆ Tollgate ⊗ WIP ▽ Critical Step ✚ Team Safety

Job Instruction Sheet

	Major Steps	Details (if applicable)	Reasons (Why)
	Brainstorm Solutions		
1	Take top root causes identified in Gap Analysis and place vertical order on flip chart.		• Need to understand the root cause(s) of the problem before you can effectively solve the problem
2	Ask team to brainstorm potential solution for identified problem, one at a time. Tips: At least 3 😊 solutions for each root cause. Tell them there are no dumb ideas and NO DISCUSSION! (Don't let the team get wrapped up in if the solution will work or not, just keep throwing out ideas) Could be done as silent brainstorm to get all ideas on table.	• Silent brainstorm can be done by having everybody write ideas on post-its and then giving them to the facilitator, instead of going around the room to have team members say ideas out loud	• Need to get ALL ideas out on the table. Even if certain ideas don't get implemented, they may spur ideas from others. • No discussion so people are more apt to throw out ideas without fear of being questioned or embarrassed • Don't go into details of solutions yet because you won't have time to discover all possible solutions
3	List all potential solutions opposite of identified problem and review with team		• Make sure everybody on the team is aware of what ideas have been put on the table
	Prioritize Solutions		
4	Prioritize solutions based on impact to metrics. Create a PICK Chart using 3M paper like the example. You will want to place each solution onto the PICK chart one at a time getting feedback from the team as to if it's High or Low Impact and then Low or High Difficulty	• Impact should be based on Impact to Metrics	• Need to prioritize to know what to work on first
5	Each solution will then fall into the categories of Possible, Implement, Challenge and Kill (spelling PICK)		
6	Use highest rated solutions for trials TIP: You will likely want to focus the group on the items in Implement area first. This helps the group focus on certain solutions before others.	• Focus on the Implement area first. • Don't even consider items in the Kill area. If an idea has low impact and is difficult to implement, there is no need to work on it	• This is where you will get the biggest gains

PICK Chart

Last Updated	XX/XX/XX	Owner		Performed By	Everyone		Work In	1
		Revised By		Rev. Number	3		Process	
Takt Time	NA	Trigger	Need to identify solutions	Done	Solutions ranked			

Process Owner Overview

	Major Steps	Work Time	Wait Time	Process Observations	Diagram, Work Flow, Picture, Time Grid
					🕐 Tip ◆ Tollgate ⊗ WIP ▽ Critical Step ✚ Team Safety
	Brainstorm Solutions				
1	Take top root causes identified in Gap Analysis and place vertical order on flip chart.				
2	Ask team to brainstorm potential solution for identified problem, one at a time. Tips: At least 3 solutions for each root cause. Tell them there are no dumb ideas and NO DISCUSSION! (Don't let the team get wrapped up in if the solution will work or not, just keep throwing out ideas) Could be done as silent brainstorm to get all ideas on table.				
3	List all potential solutions opposite of identified problem and review with team				
	Prioritize Solutions				
4	Prioritize solutions based on impact to metrics. Create a PICK Chart using 3M paper like the example. You will want to place each solution onto the PICK chart one at a time getting feedback from the team as to if it's High or Low Impact and then Low or High Difficulty				
5	Each solution will then fall into the categories of Possible, Implement, Challenge and Kill (spelling PICK)				
6	Use highest rated solutions for trials TIP: You will likely want to focus the group on the items in Implement area first. This helps the group focus on certain solutions before others.				

Notes

Introduction

1. Institute of Medicine (1999).
2. James (2013).
3. Toussaint and Gerard (2010).

Chapter 1

1. Lean Enterprise Institute.org (2015).
2. Gawande (2010).
3. Toyotakentucky.com (2015).
4. Barnas (2014).

Chapter 2

1. Pande (2013).
2. Crosby (1979).
3. Gawande (2010).
4. Rother and Shook (2009).
5. See Hospital Compare, http://www.medicare.gov/hospitalcompare/profile. html#profTab=1&ID=521326&state=WI&lat=0&lng=0&name=ThedaCar e&Distn=0.0 (accessed January 16, 2015).
6. Rother and Shook (2009).

Chapter 3

1. Mann (n.d.).
2. Mann (n.d.).
3. Mindtools.com (2015).
4. Mindtools.com (2015).
5. Hunter (1998).
6. Hunter (1998).
7. Mindtools.com (2015).
8. Createvalue.org (2015).

References

Akram, B., and C. Joseph. 2007. "Building, Maintaining and Recovering Trust: A Core Leadership Competency." FPO. http://www.freepatentsonline.com/article/Physician-Executive/158957561.html

Barnas, K. May 2014. *Beyond Heroes*. ThedaCare Center for Healthcare Value.

Createvalue.org. 2015 Clinical Business Intelligence Network. http://createvalue.org/networks/clinical-business-intelligence-network/ (accessed January 16).

Crosby, P.B. 1979. *Quality Is Free: The Art of Making Quality Certain*. New York, NY: McGraw-Hill.

Gawande, A. 2010. *The Checklist Manifesto: How to Get Things Right*. New York, NY: Metropolitan Books.

Hunter, J.C. 1998. *The Servant: A Simple Story About the True Essence of Leadership*. Rocklin, CA: Prima Pub.

Institute of Medicine. 1999. *To Err Is Human: Building a Safer Health System*. Washington, DC: National Academy Press. https://www.iom.edu/~/media/Files/Report%20Files/1999/To-Err-is-Human/To%20Err%20is%20Human%201999%20%20report%20brief.pdf

James, J.T. 2013. "A New, Evidence-Based Estimate of Patient Harms Associated with Hospital Care." *Journal of Patient Safety*. 9, no. 3, pp. 122–28. http://journals.lww.com/journalpatientsafety/Fulltext/2013/09000/A_New,_Evidence_based_Estimate_of_Patient_Harms.2.aspx

Lean Enterprise Institute.org. 2015. What Is Lean? http://www.lean.org/whatslean/ (accessed on February 15, 2015).

Mann, D. n.d. *Creating a Lean Culture*.

Mindtools.com. 2015. "Bridges Transition Model." http://www.mindtools.com/pages/article/bridges-transition-model.htm (accessed January 16, 2015).

Pande, R. 2013. "Cholesterol and Statins: It's No Longer Just About the Numbers." *Harvard Health Blog*. https://www.health.harvard.edu/blog/cholesterol-and-statins-its-no-longer-just-about-the-numbers-201311136868

Rother, M., and J. Shook. June 2009. *Learning to See Value-Stream Mapping and Eliminate Muda*. Cambridge, MA: The Lean Enterprise Institute.

Toussaint, J., and R.A. Gerard. 2010. *On the Mend: Revolutionizing Healthcare to Save Lives and Transform the Industry*. Cambridge, MA: The Lean Enterprise Institute.

Toyotakentucky.com. 2015. Toyota Quality. http://www.toyotageorgetown.com/qualdex.asp (accessed January 1, 2015).

Index

OTHER TITLES IN OUR HEALTH CARE MANAGEMENT COLLECTION

David Dilts, Oregon Health & Science University (OHSU)
and Lawrence Fredendall, Clemson University, Editors

- *Healthcare Supply Chain Management: Basic Concepts and Principles* by Hokey Min

FORTHCOMING TITLES IN THIS COLLECTION

- *Leading Teams in Healthcare Organizations* by Chris Johnson and Kurt O'Brien
- *Improving Healthcare Management at the Top: How Balanced Boardrooms Can Lead to Organizational Success* by Milan Frankl and Sharon Roberts

Business Expert Press has over 30 collection in business subjects such as finance, marketing strategy, sustainability, public relations, economics, accounting, corporate communications, and many others. For more information about all our collections, please visit www.businessexpertpress.com/collections.

Announcing the Business Expert Press Digital Library

Concise e-books business students need for classroom and research

This book can also be purchased in an e-book collection by your library as

- a one-time purchase,
- that is owned forever,
- allows for simultaneous readers,
- has no restrictions on printing, and
- can be downloaded as PDFs from within the library community.

Our digital library collections are a great solution to beat the rising cost of textbooks. E-books can be loaded into their course management systems or onto students' e-book readers.
The **Business Expert Press** digital libraries are very affordable, with no obligation to buy in future years. For more information, please visit **www.businessexpertpress.com/librarians**. To set up a trial in the United States, please email **sales@businessexpertpress.com**.

CPSIA information can be obtained
at www.ICGtesting.com
Printed in the USA
LVHW03s0259140718
583682LV00007B/28/P

9 781606 499788